BETWEEN THE POLES

LARRY LEE

LifeRich
PUBLISHING

LifeRich Publishing books may be ordered through booksellers or by contacting:

LifeRich Publishing
1663 Liberty Drive
Bloomington, IN 47403
www.liferichpublishing.com
1 (888) 238-8637

ISBN: 978-1-4897-1404-6 (sc)
ISBN: 978-1-4897-1405-3 (hc)
ISBN: 978-1-4897-1403-9 (e)

Library of Congress Control Number: 2017956020

Print information available on the last page.

LifeRich Publishing rev. date: 10/25/2017

PREFACE

At the ripe old age of 72, retired but active, I decided (with much encouragement from friends and family) to take my notes, pictures, and memories, and put them into "book" form. Not an autobiography, rather a "period" journal of who, what, when, why and what-for epilogue of my four glamorous and adventurous years in the United States Navy. It was during this period of time that I was transformed from a smart ass kid into a hard-working, tax-paying young adult. It would do well for all of our young men and women to spend time in the military where they would learn respect, dedication and self-esteem that is sadly needed in the world today.

This book stems from keeping a daily log of my experiences in and with "Operation Deepfreeze 63" aboard the U.S.S. Staten Island (AGB-5). What possessed me to keep a journal is still not known; what kept me keeping the journal is still not known; and why I still, to this day, have that journal is still not known. What I do know is, without it, this book would have never happened. The journal is now well over 52 years old, ragged and worn, but holds an adventure that in itself could be a novel and one hell of an interesting movie.

Much of what is written in these pages comes from the vast locker called my brain, pictures, the internet, and contacts I have made with past shipmates.

I have made a very calculated effort to refer to shipmates and others, not by name but by initials or nick-names. Some are no longer with us, and many I was unable to locate even with the "worldwide web." They are all part of this experience that I call "Between The Poles."

I do this with thanks to my best friend, wife and travel companion, Carol; my past shipmates; to all my friends who have encouraged me to put this on paper; and to my children, grandchildren, and other family members who have endured the endless stories told over and over.

Every effort has been made to make this as accurate as possible and with as little embellishment as possible, and for me…that is very difficult.

I also want to thank Kodak as without their film I would not have been able to capture the hundreds of photos that helped put things in order and give credence to this story.

I want to pay special thanks to those who have served prior to, during and since my time in the United States Navy. The sacrifices that so many have made can and should never be forgotten as they and their families have paid the ultimate price for your freedom. May God bless them and this great country.

CHAPTER 1

BETWEEN THE POLES

At some point in one's life, decisions must be made. Mine came during my middle years in high school, late in my sophomore or early junior years. I was not happy, although I had a darling little belle for a girlfriend and great buddies. We were all at that stage of dreaming about what was in front of us and just what we had to do to make it happen. For many, college was next with bright futures on the horizon. For others, not so much; too much doubt, anxiety or frustration. Mine was all three.

My parents divorced when I was six and my life began with a tumble that lasted several years. According to the divorce papers, which were recovered when my dad passed away in 1984, I had been awarded to my father, and my little brother was under the domicile of our mother. Now, my dad was not and never was ready for child-caring, so I was passed on to my great aunt and uncle who had raised him after his parents died when he was 12. So at this point in my young life, the future was planned for me...and, boy, was I in for a surprise.

Growing up we all had rules and I am okay with rules. We all have to pay consequences for not obeying those rules, some more than others...that was me! I was not physically abused, I was not starved, I was not deprived, I was not beaten; however, I was introduced to Mr. Belt. Growing up in a very nice home in an up-scale neighborhood in Kansas City, I went to nice schools, so on the surface one would think this kid had it made. Most everyone thought I was A-okay.

Things were not A-okay, as I lived with threats - threats that scared the crap out of me, things I just don't need to put into words at this point, but please know that they had a profound effect on me for many years. I knew I had to leave this situation as soon as possible. These threats came from my aunt, and to this day I do not believe my uncle even knew it was happening.

After graduation in 1960, I headed to the Kansas City Community College. I was young, 17, and still had no idea of what I really wanted to do. Being good at drafting, I thought architecture was perfect for me and so the future was on course. In one of my classes was another lost soul, Mike C. We became good friends right away, and although our younger days were entirely different, we both had the same feelings. Mike, also 17, was not really ready for college and with the political climate being what it was in early 1960, we knew we must join the service or be drafted! I was not going to wear a tie or sleep in dirt, and Mike, having been raised an Air Force brat, was not ready to spend the next four years doing what his dad had done.

Knowing that I had to wait until I was 18 to join (legal age, no way to stop me now), we waited until my birthday, October 28, and then made the trip to the recruiting offices in downtown Kansas City, MO. They were all in a row, and as we passed the Army, Air Force and Marine Corps offices, we kindly waved and stopped at the Navy to see what we could see. And the future began that day. As we needed to finish the semester, Mike and I chose Feb 3, 1961, along with several other lost souls, as our day to say "I do!"

So as of this point my future has been decided by me, not someone else! I can remember feeling very excited and proud as I was going to serve my country, see the world and even grow up a little. But I had one more major step to perform before the grand event started…telling my aunt and uncle of my BOLD MOVE!

Mike of course went home and told his parents, informed them that a signature was needed as he was still 17, and then they all celebrated. Me, well it was a little more stressful than that! My stomach was in knots, I was sweating bullets, and at one point before arriving home, I considered just moving in with Mike and not telling them at all…I would just mail them a letter from San Diego.

I chose to wait until after dinner while my aunt and uncle finished their last cups of coffee. This was like the "last supper" before a hanging! To this day I have no idea what was for supper and I'm sure I upchucked it later anyway. After we had finished, I pushed my chair back from the table and announced that I had something important to tell them. My uncle, smart as he was, knew that something big was about to happen so he got up and poured himself another cup of joe, sat back down and said: "let's have it." GULP!

I was now on stage and I knew it had to be good, so I let loose. "I joined the Navy today." The reaction was immediate as I knew it would be. "You can't do that! I won't let it happen!" was the noise that came from my aunt. I looked at my uncle then back to my aunt and said, "Well, I signed the papers today and being 18, there really isn't much you can do about it." My heart was pounding right out of my chest cavity, but at this point I was gaining a little courage. Again in my aunt's sternest words, she vowed to stop it. Now my uncle, who was always calm and mostly listened, said, "Fay, shut up!" Now two of us have our balls in a vise and I was not sure who would be first to feel the pinch. My uncle continued, "Larry has made his mind up about this, he's of age and I support him 100%!" Old Aunt Fay at 5 ft and 95 lbs would not back down from Godzilla, but she clammed up and just started to cry. The hard part was over.

The next few months were filled with many, many thoughts coupled with anxiety and concern. Had I done the right thing? Was I out of my mind? But the future was calling and I couldn't wait. My aunt was constantly questioning my choices and it was obvious she had come to the realization that there really wasn't a damn thing she could do about it. Thanksgiving, then Christmas and New Years came and went, and February 3 was right around the corner.

I spent as much time as possible with my girl, and I think we both knew this would be the end of our relationship as she would graduate in the spring and head to the University of Missouri where she surely would be hotly pursued. But she was always on my mind for many months to come.

I was up before the crack of dawn on Feb 3, 1961. Little did I know, that was going to be the daily norm for many months to come, more like 4:00 a.m. if you were lucky and earlier if the DI had a bug up his ass! Bags packed with the bare (and I mean bare) essentials, we headed to the airport where Mike and his family and my aunt and uncle met for the first time. We went to the meeting room assigned to us, and along with several other recruits and their families, we were officially sworn in. Many tears were shed and I think my aunt was the leader of the pack. After our goodbyes, we boarded a TWA constellation for our venture to San Diego.

Now at this junction of my life, I had only been on one airplane ride, and that was a jet and during daylight. This baby we were on was a prop-job and flying at night. It took me about 5 minutes to realize that the damn thing was on fire and so noted that information to the stewardess. She informed me that those flames coming off the engines were merely exhaust fumes and everything was ok. Well my shorts weren't ok, that's for sure. Wow, first day and I have already learned something new. This is going to be great!

We headed east to St. Louis to board a MSTS (military) flight with more lost souls from the Detroit area. After spending the night in a motel, we all (about 40 dudes) boarded our flight to paradise. Little did we know that these guys were going to be part of our boot camp company.

Arriving in San Diego, we were herded onto a bus and off to the San Diego Naval Training Center (SDNTC) where we would spend 14 weeks enjoying the sunshine. Now if you believe that, I have 40 acres of good swamp land I'll sell you for just a few bucks. At this point it seemed like this was a walk in the park; then we went thru the gates of hell! I thought my aunt could yell, but she couldn't hold a match to these guys. In less than five minutes, our sexuality had been challenged, our family tree, our next of kin, and our future children if we survived. What could possibly go wrong with this introduction to military life? I thought a spring vacation was awaiting our arrival, not this motley crew.

The top country hits of the time: Walk on by, Don't Worry, Hello Walls. The Top 40 hits of the time: Let's Twist Again, Stand by Me, Surrender, Hello Mary Lou.

CHAPTER 2

BOOT CAMP

February, 1961. Day one of boot camp started with a jolt of reality. Yelling, name-calling, degradation, and just plain good old-fashioned military bull shit! The petty officers in charge started passing out orders faster than Pinocchio can lie. Do this...do that...stand at attention...right face...left face...shoulders back...eyes straight ahead...etc, etc, etc. I think you get the message. Ninety-six percent of these poor souls have no idea how to handle all of this. Fortunately for me, I had attended Wentworth Military Academy my eighth and ninth grades so I really had this part of the program down just about pat. I knew how to march, I kinda' knew how to shut my mouth…well, maybe not so much...and I was totally aware at this point to do just as they said. There were two others in our company who had some military experience, so that was 3 out of 80 who had a little edge on day one.

Like a herd of sheep, we were marched for about fifteen minutes to a barracks that was going to be our temporary home for the first week, after which we would be outfitted, hair cut, inoculated with shots for things I had never heard of and shots in places I did not know I had, dentistry, swimming…a sailor must be able to swim…and most importantly, indoctrination. What a week to look forward to.

We were introduced to our DI and company commander, a Chief Petty Officer who would be our leader for the duration of this little adventure. He would teach all the fine arts of being fine upstanding sailors.

Note: I will always refer to a barracks as a barn because it reminds me of an old barn but has no animals with fur or feathers, just bunks, lockers and the "head." The "head" is Navy talk for bathroom and one must never call it a bathroom while in the Navy or Marine Corps.

As we entered the barn we were told to grab a bunk. Now for most of these guys that was the clue to take a nap. Wrong! We put what meager belongings we had into a locker and it was back out for yet another march. This time the barbers were waiting for us. There were haircuts from duck-tails to flat-tops and everything in-between. It took all of about 90 seconds to get your first free hair cut; boy, did we all look cute. Some heads were bleeding but all survived. Up next, outfitting.

Another barn-like building and in we go. Single file in what looked like a never-ending line. Socks (white and black), skivvies (military for underwear), three white uniforms, one blue dress uniform, belt, shoes, boots, sneakers, night watch gear, a Donald Duck hat, white hats, a Petty coat and a duffle bag. Most of the gear was issued in sixes, six pairs of skivvy boxers, skivvy shirts, socks, white and dress uniforms included pants and jumpers, and singletons of everything else. Now this is a lot of crap, and we are carrying all of this in our arms. The next table was for marking your name in each piece of your new wardrobe. Stencils were made for each man, last name first, comma first name. Piece by piece, one by one, each and every item was so marked. Once through that line we are told to strip out of our civilian clothes, butt-naked, and get dressed in our new, bright shiny duds. White boxers, white t-shirt, white pants, white jumper, black socks, boots, and topped off with a sailor's trademark - the white hat!

We soon found out that the military has some flaws. One of course is sizing correctly. I was one of the lucky ones and I was considered to be of normal size - 6'2" and 178 lbs - perfect. Mike was also so blessed as were several others. But those who showed up a tad on the LARGE size were issued clothes that you would be wearing after they finished with you in 14 weeks and the skinny ones were issued clothes that you would grow into. They had a plan and, believe it or not, it really worked. Diet, exercise and not much sleep made you fit the mold. Now we were instructed on how to put 80-lbs of crap into a 50-lb bag a.k.a. duffle. In the military there is a right way and wrong way to fold clothes and we are now being taught that procedure. All stuffed into the duffle, we now had to haul this back to the barn. It would have been nice of them to provide vehicles to get there but I guess they wanted us to break in our new shiny boots right away.

At this point we were beginning to look like sailors. Some short, some tall, some skinny and a few large, and in just about 14 weeks we would all be in great shape and ready to head to the fleet, but we had to get through this week. Before we started the training process, we had to get through the "do it like we want" week and it has already started the stress process, and for those "special" few, it was going to be an unforgettable experience.

No matter what event was ahead of you, it was a 2-mile hike. I think they planned it that way. At the end of boot camp most of us tossed our boots away as they were completely shot, worn out from walking and running 7 days a week for 14 weeks. Think about it, you could walk across America and still have some mileage on your boots. I will admit that just after a couple of days, those damn boots fit like a glove and really were quite comfortable. I'm still trying to figure out just how far we really walked and ran during those 14 weeks.

Each day we attended some sort of classroom instructions and were provided with an array of books and/or literature that would teach us how to be good sailors and servicemen. And believe me, we were tested daily. You MUST know the chain of command from the President down to the lowest piss-ant just above you. Since you are the lowest piece of shit on the planet at this point, you had to know everybody, their position or rank and who they were sleeping with. The military code of conduct was another test of one's brain, but that also had to be ingrained into the skull...and quickly. Books on knots, sailor words, military rank and rate of all branches of service, types of ships...what happened to our vacation?

The week went by quickly. We were getting to know one another and the pecking order was established. One thing we had to do was choose our Boot Company Commander, and for us that was a no-brainer. One of three guys from a small town in Kentucky had been in the Army for a short time, and when the other two decided to join the Navy, he transferred. He was a great guy and helped all of us with the reality of what we were going through.

One would ask, 'why does it take 14 weeks to train someone to be a sailor', and after the first week that question was asked daily. One week was nothing but fire-fighting...that was the toughest week of all. It was dirty, stressful, smelly, and down-right hard work. Keep in mind, there is no 911 on board a ship so everyone must have some knowledge of what in the hell to do if your ship is on fire. Since then, I have had 100% respect for those who choose to be firemen; they earn every penny they're paid.

After our temporary barn, it was off to Nimitz Island for a 4-week stay in what was called "quarantine," because all the shots and meds we were given could cause just about every known malady in the world and they wanted to separate you from those that had been cured...RIGHT! I think it was to make us walk all that much farther every day just to break in those damn boots.

Monday thru Saturday, each day started the same. Rise and shine at 4:00 a.m., and for the next 4 hours you prepared yourself for inspection, studied if you needed to, went to chow, cleaned the barn, and then lined up for muster at 0730 (that's 7:30 a.m. for you civilians). We then went off to the grinder where you and thousands of others went to practice graduation. Yes, you read correctly, graduation! All lined up, company after company in their clean white uniforms and rifles at their sides, we awaited 0800 and the rising of the "ensign," our nations flag. Roll-call was made, then inspection, and any unshined boots or "filthy" items were so noted. We then proceeded with our daily drill. This preparation for graduation was nothing more than a formalized exercise program that included a 9 lb rifle. We did this routine 6 days a week for 13 weeks. The whole process took about an hour and was, of course, about two miles away from anything... funny how they figured that out.

For clarification, there are several words in the military that make no sense to civilians...hell, some of them make no sense to those of us who had to use them. "Grinder" for example is nothing more than a large slab of concrete or blacktop that covers acres and is used for such nonsense as getting ready for graduation. More examples of strange words - a hat is a cover, a floor is a deck, a mop is a swab, a wall is a bulkhead, a ceiling is an overhead, and the list goes on and on. I will try to clarify as new ones are introduced.

"Filthy" on the other hand means the same to both parties here; however, what civilians consider filthy and what it means in boot camp are planets away from one another. There are many words that will appear in this journal and if I fail to explain, please forgive me.

Each week brought more surprises, testing and growth. Swimming was early on, and no, it was not a trip to the beach. Each recruit must pass the swimming test, then the survival test. Having learned the correct art of swimming at an early age, I thought this would be a joke. There were about a dozen or so of our lost souls who could not pass this test. Some damn-near drowned, so were separated from us while we continued. Those who did not pass went to swimming lessons in another pool and would continue lessons until they could pass the test. The rest of us were told to get dressed and return to the pool deck. What? The instructor then proceeded to give us the drill about the design of the naval uniform and its many advantages. Then came the words we knew were coming! JUMP IN! Fully dressed, in we went. You had two minutes to get out of your jumper and pants, then make a flotation device and successfully float. You soon discover why the jumper is not tucked into your pants and why the pants have that bell-bottom feature. We all have gotten caught in a down-pour and were completely soaked...yep, hard to get the clothes off especially if you have your shoes on. Trying to undress, treading water so you don't drown, tying the legs of your pants into knots, then proceeding to get air into those pants all within two minutes was hysterical at least. Now typical military here…if the group has one idiot, then "do-overs" apply. In this group we had three who just couldn't get the message, but we were all finally through after three attempts.

Another glorious day was the trip to the dentist. The Navy wants everyone to have bright shiny, decay-free teeth for all the girls to see, so they make sure you fit the mold. Again, I got lucky...not that I had or have great teeth but my aunt insisted on a trip to the dentist prior to my departure to San Diego so I was out of the dentist's office in a flash; however, some of the guys had no idea what they were in for. After an examination, the dentist would make his decision to fix or remove, and if enough needed removal…well, goodbye teeth. Removal was not nice! Some of these poor slobs went in with teeth and came out with just gums and would receive their new military-issued teeth in about a week. The looks on the faces of the toothless was priceless; stunned, shocked, scared, and forlorn come to mind. But again, by graduation all would be good and forgotten.

Having tested well at the recruiting office, I was not concerned with the testing done during boot camp. There were two days of solid testing of just about every aptitude you can think of and the results of those tests will guide you to a "rate;" i.e. ET Electronic Technician, RD Radarman, YM Yeoman, and so on. If your test results are not good, you are sent to the fleet without further schooling and are placed in departments on an as-need basis, so paying attention during these batteries of tests was extremely important. If memory serves me right, I believe there were at least twelve different tests. There were two tests that aimed at your hearing and response. One was Morse code; the other was sonar pings. A few letters would be sounded out...A then dit dah, S dit dit dit, U dit dit dah, N dah dit, then the code would play back in random order and you had to select the correct corresponding letter. This test lasted about 30 minutes and incorporated most of the alphabet. When finished, most wanted to scream. Again I was lucky as I had learned a little of the Morse code concept while in the Boy Scouts and it helped. The.same scenario applied for sonar. I felt I scored well in both tests. I was guaranteed a rating in electronics due to my pre-testing and I would later learn why I became an RM Radioman. My buddy Mike would become a HM Hospital Corpsman (medic). Tons of stress was put on us during this testing period as your DI wanted to have the smartest company, and if the DI didn't get what he wanted there was always hell to pay. Testing results would come weeks later and most couldn't wait to find out what, where and how they would spend their days in the U.S. Navy.

After the four weeks on Nimitz Island, we headed to our new barn and continued walking/running our asses off, practicing graduation, going to classes and doing our daily washing clothes, studying, getting mail, writing letters, and of course talking about our first "liberty." After seven weeks of "boot" and if the DI grants it, we would be allowed to put on our finest and head into San Diego for a little R & R (rest & recreation). After being confined for eight weeks, that day couldn't have come sooner. Most were allowed liberty in our company, and Mike and I caught the bus. Downtown San Diego, here we come. Where do you go first? Well, for Mike it was the tattoo parlor at which I questioned his mentality but it was something he wanted to do. After getting his devil on his shoulder, we just wandered around looking at the sights, and buying post cards and trinkets to send home. This much-needed time away from SDNTC was short-lived and we soon found ourselves back at the barn getting ready for the next six weeks. We would have another day like this before graduation; that is, if everything went well.

About a week before graduation our DI called a meeting in the barn and he read all the results of our testing and where each of us was headed when this was over. Anxiously awaiting your name to be called and applauding those that were headed for great duty, the tension grew. Finally the DI yelled "LEE" and informed me that I was headed to Radioman "A" school and at none other than SDNTC. Great, I would be spending 6 more months at the other end of this giant base. Mike was headed to Corps School at Balboa Naval Hospital at the other side of San Diego so we would at least get to see each other for the next few months. I was headed to Radioman school with another member of our company, one of the three Kentucky boys, and he and I became good friends.

Graduation day came and excitement was at a peak, but friendships would end, and unknowns again faced each and every one of us. We all got our next stripe and now were Seaman Apprentice (E-2) grade except for the Army guy from Kentucky who became a Seaman (E-3).

The next day I headed back home for a two-week leave. An early flight out of San Diego and before I knew it, there I was back in Kansas City. Waiting were my aunt & uncle, my little belle, and a whole gaggle of friends that just couldn't wait to see me in a sailor suit. If only the weeks in boot camp would have flown by as fast as these two did. Before I knew it, I was back in San Diego getting ready to be trained to be a Radioman.

Note: During boot camp, law and order is not only governed by the DI but the boots themselves must make things happen. When one individual causes the group to suffer, action must take place. This action is overlooked by the DI if it does not get out of hand. For example, Johnny consistently cannot pass inspection due to filthiness so Johnny must get a lesson in cleanliness. Now we learn a new military phrase: "GI" Shower." A GI shower usually happens after taps. The appointed committee, usually about four to five fellow boots, grab Johnny and take him to the head where another committee awaits with scrub brushes and soap. After about a five-minute lesson on cleanliness, Johnny normally learns this fine art. If "do-overs" are needed, the next shower is more severe and may require a trip to sick-bay.

Another example of such extra education is referred to as the "Blanket Party." This will usually only take one lesson. Any individual who continues to cause the whole company to suffer due to lack of paying attention to detail can be awarded with this surprise. Again, an appointed committee of about eight boots would gather after everyone is asleep and very quietly surround the dead-beat in his bunk. Two grab arms and two grab feet, and the rest beat the crap out of him with those hard-soled flip-flops we were issued week one. These flip flops were like old tires, very hard, and will put a welt on bare skin that most won't soon forget. The final step usually requires a "fall down the stairs" method of education.

Our company had only two who could not get the grip on reality. Both received GI Showers with one having two "do-overs" before he got the message. The other one not only got the GI shower but he also received the Blanket Party, and for that we made sure he stayed in place so he could get a good whoopin'. We made a rope out of our "clothes ties" and roped him to his bed before the education began. This way he was not going to get up until we were ready to quit.

For the record, during Navy boot camp, one does his laundry every day on a concrete slab, wearing his flip flops, with a bucket of water, a bar of soap, and the infamous scrub brush. When done, those clothes are hung on a clothes line inside out with "clothes ties" with the correct knot and with the "fly" facing the Marine Boot Camp. "Piss on the Marines" is how we were instructed. Those ties were about 12 inches in length so it took dozens to make a rope to surround our student.

The laundry was so valuable that a guard with their unloaded weapon was required to stand watch over it from "taps" to "revelry." Two-hour watches were done by all, walking around those damn clothes the whole two hours.

The top country hits of the time: North to Alaska, I Fall to Pieces, Sea of Heartbreak. The top 40 hits of the time: Wooden Heart, Blue Moon, Runaway, Michael Row the Boat.

CHAPTER 3

RADIOMAN SCHOOL

My short visit home was filled with many memories, good home cooked meals, dates with my belle, hanging with my friends, and answering thousands of questions about what I had been through and where I was headed. I would come to miss these moments very quickly; however, I have many memories I will never forget. Trying to become a man isn't easy; it takes time and effort. I hoped that I was prepared for the challenges ahead.

This trip to San Diego was certainly different than the first. Standing among many of the same friends and family all dressed up in my new dress uniform, I realized I truly was now on my own. I'm not traveling with others in the same boat and I have no one to rely on but myself. I have to make the decisions that will get me to the SDNTC by 0800 in the morning including a plane change in L.A. Thank God everything went well. I was on time and ready to face the new challenge.

Upon arrival at SDNTC, I was taken to yet another barn to drop my duffle and other personal items. Then off to the admin building of the radioman school and assigned to a class that would start in less than two weeks. A 3rd class Petty Officer showed me around the facility and then back to the barn, and I was told to await further orders. In the military, orders are always around the corner so one does not have to wait long, as they can and will find something for you to do without much thought process.

Shortly after that, my boot camp pal, Dale, from Kentucky showed up and we started to get to know one another and shared our experiences of going back home as a brand-new shiny sailor. He was married and was awaiting the arrival of his wife and little baby girl. Once they arrived his freedom would be limited so we did not get much time to explore civilian life outside these walls. We did start meeting many of our future classmates, some just out of boot camp like ourselves, and others who had been in the reserves and were now going on active duty.

Dale had married his high school sweetheart right after they graduated. Upon arriving in San Diego, they rented a small apartment just outside the base. This guy really had a lot on his plate.

Mike and I had hooked up via telephone and planned to meet in downtown San Diego on Saturday, take a bus to the beach and chase the chicks. Wow, our first real liberty and it was just a few days away. The anticipation was overwhelming. We met at the YMCA in downtown San Diego, talked about our two weeks' leave and made our plans for the day. First was getting a locker for our civilian clothes as they were not allowed to be stored in the barn. Not very expensive, they reminded me of the locker room at school, only much bigger. We changed clothes and were off to the beach.

There aren't many beaches in Kansas City, just pools and lakes, so this trip to the beach was a real treat. Totally unprepared for the California sun and being as fair as a peeled radish, it took me a grand total of about 30 minutes to get fried. Mike had grown up in Texas and spent lots of time on the gulf beaches. He kept telling me I was getting burned but I wouldn't listen. With the ocean breeze and the desire to get a tan, I really didn't get the feeling I was being prepared for serving. After much coaxing by Mike, we finally boarded the bus for the long ride back to our lockers. Once on board the bus I began to feel my skin getting tight. Now I had been sunburned before and I knew the feeling, but I had never been "fried."

Once at our locker, we hopped into the showers and that's when I knew I was in TROUBLE. I now looked like that radish before it got peeled. My shoulders, back and legs were well done! We said goodbye and headed to our respective bases. I started feeling really ill and not realizing that I was not only totally burned, I was dehydrated. That night seemed to never end. Shaking like a leaf in a wind storm and going from hot to cold, I prayed for morning so I could get to the chow hall.

Although the weather was on the hot side of warm, we were still in "winter dress" so our blue wool uniforms were in order. It felt like the largest piece of sandpaper was being applied to my poor body, and I was about to lose my breakfast and I hadn't even eaten yet. Again, walking was the mode of transport, and a mile and a half was in front of me. I was so sore, so stiff and so sick, I thought I would never get there, and once there I would have to make the trek back to the barn for 0800 muster.

After muster some of us were taken to the radioman school for clean-up duty. I could barely move and was ready to go back home to Kansas City so my aunt could take care of me...I was miserable. Again, luck found me in the form of the 3rd Class Petty Officer who showed me around on the first day. He opened the door to the office and said "come in here!" Oops, what did I do? Once inside and the door shut, he proceeded to scare the living crap out of me with threats of being court-martialed under one of the articles of military justice. Of course I had learned those articles in boot but I had no idea what in the hell he was talking about. By the look on my face, he knew I had no idea what he was talking about. "DESTRUCTION OF GOVERNMENT PROPERTY, ASS-HOLE!" came bellowing out of his mouth. Yep, I was GOVERNMENT PROPERTY and I had fried it! Now is when the luck came to me. The office was air-conditioned and somewhat private with a good view of the courtyard. He knew I was in trouble and he had also suffered the same malady early in his navy days. He went to a closet, retrieved a bucket and mop, filled the bucket with water, pulled up a chair and informed me to "sit your ass down" and said "if anyone approaches the office, get up and start mopping the deck." I was a mopping fool for the whole week, in air-conditioning and sitting on my posterior! To this day, every time

I'm in the sun a little too long, I think of him and could never ever thank him enough.

Note: Punitive Article 108 of the Uniformed Code of Military Justice is defined as: Destruction of Government Property. Any military person is subject to this chapter who, without proper authority – 1. Sells or disposes of; 2. Willfully or through neglect, damages, destroys, or loses; or 3. Willfully or through neglect suffers to be lost, damaged, destroyed, sold, or wrongfully disposed of, any military property of the United States, shall be punished as a court-martial may direct." In other words, getting sunburned to the point of not being able to perform your duties could put one in position to be charged under this Article.

I could not get under the shower head as the pain was like a thousand needles being driven into my fried skin. I longed for a bath tub but that luxury is not afforded at this level of military service. I bathed out of a sink for a week. Then, news of another move to yet another barn, our officially assigned Radioman A School barn...and yes, it was two miles away. I packed that damn duffle and began to lug it to the new home. Most would throw it on their shoulder and head off. I was so sore I could hardly stand wind blowing on me let alone throw a canvas duffle filled with 80 pounds of carefully folded clothes over my shoulder. So off I went, at a snail's gait, dragging that godforsaken bag behind me. At this pace I should arrive at the new barn in about two days.

Once again luck found me. Was I living a dream? Halfway through my journey, this long black, limo-like car with flags on each fender pulled alongside me and came to a stop. The rear window came down and this woman asked, "Are you okay?"

Now, I'm a newbie at this gig but I knew what those flags were for and it wasn't a taxi service. That car belonged to the base commander, a two-star admiral, and this was his wife. OH CRAP, DESTRUCTION OF GOVERNMENT PROPERTY hit me right between the ears. I quickly announced, "I'm fine, thank you ma'am."

Anyone looking at me knew I was full of shit. I was fried and one could not hide that! I was walking like a duck, what skin was showing still looked like that radish, and I had LIAR written across my forehead. She then proceeded to "order" me into the limo and had the driver put my duffle in the trunk.

"Where are you headed sailor?"

Barracks # (I dare not say "barn" and for the life of me I do not remember that number).

En route she informed me that it was obvious I was fried and began to instruct me in the art of taking care of it.

"When you get to the barracks, get into the shower room (each barrack's shower rooms have about 20 spouts…lots of privacy), turn on ALL the showers as hot as possible and get it steaming in there. Then get under one of those showers set at a comfort level for you and stay in there for about 10 minutes."

She had just created my own personal sauna and by God it worked. Once at the barn she gave me her calling card and said, "If anyone gives you grief over the shower treatment, just have them call me!"

I thanked her for her kindness and said goodbye. Of course once in the shower room soothing my fried skin, the barn petty officer in charge had a major stroke but after I gave him the card, I never heard another word about it. That woman saved my ass! It took about three weeks before I felt anything like normal, but the pain almost immediately decreased and I was on the mend. When will my luck run out…?

We started class in mid May of '61 and would graduate mid November - 26 weeks of Morse code and electronics ahead of us. Day in and day out for 26 weeks it was 2 hours of code, smoke break, 2 hours electronics, 1 hour lunch break, 2 hours of code, smoke break, 2 hours electronics. After just two weeks of this, one no longer read anything normally…it was dits and dahs till you couldn't think straight. Guys would even communicate in code: "dit dah dah, dit dit dit dit, dit dah, dah" "dah, dit dit dit dit, dit" "dit dit dah dit, dit dit dah, dah dit dah dit, dah dit dah." Really!

Learning the code was like learning a language. It was repetitious until you mastered the alphabet, punctuation and numbers, then one had to master the speed. You sat at a manual typewriter that was all uppercase with earphones on your head and you went through reams and reams of paper. After passing the testing for learning the language, you moved on to speed. At first it was easy, each day one improved and early on it was fun. Then as speed got faster, 6 words a minute, those dits and dahs began to run together and that's when things started slowing down. A word is described as a grouping of five coded letters and/or numbers. Once received, those groups could be decoded into English.

Once the 6 words a minute was reached, most of us struggled and it took all week before testing just to find out you didn't make it. That meant back after the dinner hour for another two more hours of dits and dahs until you could pass the 6 word a minute test. The next plateaus were 8, 10, 12, etc, etc., with each level needing to be passed before you moved on, and the longer it took, the farther behind you got. I struggled with 6 for about a week, then, like magic, it appeared in the brain and Bingo...I passed, then 12 words a minute was my next problem but after a few nights of extra dits and dahs, I passed that level.

As a Radioman, you not only have to receive code, you must be able to send it. It is a skill that requires flexibility, and without that you might as well hit the key with a hammer. I mastered the key right away and the summer of '63, after lots of experience, I got my speed key operator's license.

The electronics side of school was about the end of me. I struggled for six months with it and somehow managed to get by. It had to have been close, but when the final testing was over, I would officially become a Radioman Seaman Apprentice and ready to head to the fleet.

The electronics portion of this school covered everything from operating the equipment to repairing it. You needed to know everything there was about resistors, capacitors and tubes, and how they interacted with one another. Then you learned how to diagnose problems and how to repair those problems. My brain really struggled with this and I totally found it boring as hell.

This rate (RM) was two-fold by design. First you were a communicator and secondly you were a repairman. Fortunately for me, my duty assignments over the next three years would be aboard ships that required heavy on operations and little on repair. Thank God for the Electronics Technicians.

After about two weeks in San Diego, both Mike and I came to the conclusion that we needed a car. Chasing chicks sucked on a bus. So the next Saturday, we hunted for our chick machine. It didn't take long to find it but now we had to solve the problem of just how to pay for it. At $92 a month, it would have taken us 12 years to save enough money for it, let alone buy gas and have enough left for chasing chicks. Mike called his parents and informed them of our find and that he needed $165 for his half of the investment. Easy for him, but I was in a bind. My aunt still had not fully gotten over me being so bold as to join the Navy without her permission, and I figured that would be a wasted call. So I made a call that I had never made before...I called my mother. After a short "how-r-u" conversation, I dropped the bomb. There was silence at the other end but I held my tongue and then, what seemed like hours, she asked where and how she could forward the money. I was prepared for that and to Western Union we went, picked up our money, and drove away in our 1953 robin-egg blue Ford Coupe. Flat head V-8, stick shift, and looking hot, we hit the streets in search of chicks.

Mike was not allowed to house a vehicle at the hospital as that was for the doctors, all officers of course, so I was in charge and parked that beauty right along the barn. Mike and I were not on the same watch rotation so our weekends together were not as frequent as he would have liked. For me it was great as I had the car and I could go anytime I wanted or needed to. We did have many memorable weekends between Tijuana and L. A. and just about every stop in between. After four months of schooling, Mike became a Hospital Corpsman and was transferred to the Memphis Naval Air Station. Although we wrote each other and called every now and then,

I never saw him again. He stayed in for 14 years, met the love of his life, got married and left the Navy. I wonder where he is now. As my luck would have it again, I got to keep the car.

Those six months taught me so many things and molded me into the determined, self-sufficient, hard head that I am. I was getting to the point where I no longer took much crap from anyone and had the feeling that I really was growing up, although there were miles of road ahead before that really happened. Gee, I learned a language, bought my first car, lost my virginity, was having fun for the first time in my life, and I wouldn't be 19 until October 28.

About two weeks before graduation, we all learned of our future destinations. Some went to ships...some to shore stations overseas and some in the USA. I was sent to the USS Cimarron AO-22. The Cimarron was a very large tanker that provided not only crude oil for ships, but also AV-GAS and JP5, which are aviation fuels needed on carriers. I was thrilled I was going to sea. That's why I joined the Navy, to see the world. Brother... would I see the world in the next three years.

After graduation I drove back to Kansas City, dropping off classmates in Phoenix, Grand Junction and Denver, Colorado, and the last one at the Greyhound bus depot in downtown Kansas City for his trip to Iowa. This trip home was to be long remembered with tire trouble, generator problems, no heater, and no snow tires or chains in snowy weather over the mountains in Colorado. But the bus service for my classmates paid for my trip back and then some as each paid for the ride.

My visit home went by so fast I hardly remember what happened. I spent as much time with my belle, but I knew when I kissed her good-bye it would be my last. I spent many hours with my aunt and uncle as they both had many questions. My aunt was over me joining and seemed quite impressed as to my personal growth. My stay was short as I had three days' drive to get back to San Diego for transport to my new assignment, which was in Japan at this point. My last day home was spent saying goodbye to my friends and my last great home-cooked meal for some time. I had only been home 8 days and it would be 25 months before I would return.

I left early for the long drive back to San Diego. With new tires and a complete check-up on the car, thanks to my uncle, I was sure everything would be great as I was going back the southern route, so what could go wrong? The old '53 Ford was aging and the generator problem was a hidden problem and would never go away. It was still there when I finally junked the beast for $25. After a few long days of driving in bad weather (yes, I hit snow in western Oklahoma & Texas) and getting the battery recharged because the generator would not do it, I arrived on time and proceeded to check-in for the next adventure.

At just 19, I had many miles of rocky roads ahead of me. That long lonely ride back to San Diego had my mind swirling. What was next? That tunnel that lay before me was very long and very dark. No light could be seen at the end and there was trouble lurking around every corner. Will I survive? Will I make good decisions and find the sought-after light? Time will always tell, and I had to wait to learn how hard it would be to find.

Back in southern California, weekends were fabulous. Beautiful beaches, gorgeous chicks, and unbelievable weather. My favorite spots were Laguna Beach, Point Loma, La Jolla, Anaheim, Hollywood and Tijuana. These spots provided a vast array of entertainment covering water sports, entertainment and chasing chicks. Besides our paltry pay, Mike and I were able to gain additional income by providing services, like transportation and products.

With our car we would make "taxi" runs from the base to downtown San Diego. The process was simple. Stop at the bus stop outside the main gate, offer rides for a fee of 25 cents, and drop them off at the YMCA. We would offer those returning to the base the same service. Our service was quick, no waiting for a bus or the many stops it would make. Three or four trips and we had gas money for the whole weekend of cruising. We, of course, were not the only ones providing this service and soon the bus company started raising hell, and even put agents at bus stops to try and catch us.

Being ever so smart, we arranged to pick up our clients at spots other than the bus stops, and it took them weeks to figure that out. Finally we got the word from the Brass. NO MORE BUS SERVICE. Ok, that revenue source just went out the window, so what can we do to replace that much-needed income.

With Tijuana just a few miles south and booze being cheap, the solution was quickly found…booze. This was dangerous for sure, but profitable if we didn't get caught. The Borders were not as secure as they are now but you still had to pass through the check points.

The back seat of the Ford would pull out and bottles of booze could be put into the springs. I did manage to get seven bottles into those springs on one run and made a huge profit. Finally, after almost being caught, I thought better of this little gold mine, and retired.

Mike and I went to Disneyland one weekend, not to check out Mickey, but what a great place to find chicks. While waiting in line for a ride, we started a conversation with two lovelies and soon the four of us were enjoying the reminder of the day at Disney. I soon would begin dating Karen, even attended her graduation from high school, and we had a great time together. But as the new school year came around, she was off to college and I was lonely again.

We did exchange letters until I finished my time in the service. My first Christmas home I received a Christmas card from her and we exchanged cards for almost 15 years. She became a CPA, was married and had children.

One of our most favorite beach hangouts was La Jolla, referred to as the "coves and caves" for obvious reasons. The cliffs towered over the incoming waves and the bay was filled with little underwater caves. One particular cliff was about 32 feet above the water and was a challenge to everyone who came there. To wear the badge of honor, one had to jump or dive off this cliff. This was easier said than done, as the waves would pound the rocks and the water would rise and fall, thus changing the depth of the water. At low tide it was suicidal. The top of the cliff was worn smooth from brave souls who would run and jump/dive or in many cases, chicken out and stop. It took me about twenty attempts before I took the plunge...once, ONLY ONCE, as when I hit the water everyone thought I had created the Yellow Sea.

Both Mike and I had friends that would join in for all the fun and we had quite a group that frolicked throughout southern California. Dave was a corpsman and joined us regularly as did radiomen Ski from Colorado, James from Iowa and Davie from Phoenix. There were others, but these guys were always ready for fun and we didn't miss much of that.

One trip took us to Hollywood. After making gas money Friday night, we headed out early Saturday. We spent a little time in Laguna Beach checking out the chicks and action, and then made it into Hollywood after dark. I had been there when I was in the sixth grade and with my GPS brain was able to motor around the city with little help. We cruised with all the other hotrods, up and down the strip, just seeing what we could see. This was the high rent district and we were definitely out of our league. As night drew to an end, we needed to find a place to catch some ZZZ's and soon found a location above Sunset Strip.

We parked the car in what looked like a little park. Soon we discovered that right below us was none other than "77 Sunset Strip." If you were born in the 1940s/1950s, you are familiar with the hit song, "Kookie, Kookie, Lend Me Your Comb." Well that's where we were. We bedded down on the lawn and in the car, and were awake at dawn. We found a gas station, cleaned up, then looked for a cheap place to grab a donut and some coffee. This little adventure finished with us at Grauman's Chinese Theatre. Hollywood was a small town back in 1962, but the hills around Hollywood were filled with mansions of some very famous stars. We had just taken the "cheap" trip through Hollywood.

We headed back to San Diego early as money was running low. About halfway back, the old Ford died, right there on Highway 101. One thing about the old cars, you could fix one with a match book, paper clip and spit. Ski was our mechanic and he soon had the carburetor off, cleaned and replaced, and we were on our way.

There were many adventures and the fun never stopped. I don't think there is enough paper to list all of them. It was fun being young and free, and we had little worries. All we needed to do was be at school Monday morning, study and play. Sometimes I wish those days would come back; I dream of them often and wake up in a cold sweat. Life was easy and we just didn't get it! Today I feel sorry for our youth as they have way too many pressures to deal with. I tried to explain it to my children, many times, but I always got that "deer in the headlights look" and I knew they just didn't get it either. I wonder if they know just how much their father struggled with his youth and the challenges he faced trying to make it better for them. They all have children now, and I think the light is starting to shine.

The top country hits of the time: Tender Years, Fooling Around, San Antonio Rose. The Top 40 hits of the time: Run Around Sue, Little Sister, Big Bad John, The Lion Sleeps Tonight.

CHAPTER 4
THE USS CIMMARON

The same old routine at this base. Check in at the gate, get directed to the personnel office, assigned to yet another barn and await further orders. I had this part down pat by now and was not surprised by anything. I soon discovered five of my classmates were here and that helped pass the time. This was a holding area for sailors and marines who were being transferred to other sectors - the South China Sea, land bases in the Orient, or other forlorn places in the world. Some would go by plane, some by ship. It just depended on when and where you were headed. Like all other bases, muster was at 0800 and they always had jobs for you to do while you waited. I got to work in the kitchen, shag golf balls at the officers' golf course, and clean "heads." The list never ended of things they could assign you to just to keep you busy. How about a beer and a lounge chair? That was not in the mix!

The six of us stayed on base just waiting for our ship to leave. None of us had enough money to have a good liberty in San Diego, so we just did our jobs during the day and went to the movies on base at night.

It was at this base that my luck ran out. It was the day before we were to board the ship that would take us to Japan. There were three civilian guys that came into the barn, and soon the loud-speaker was calling my name.

What could they possibly want with me? When I arrived at the office, I was told to pack my duffle and follow these three dudes.

After a short drive, we arrived at what looked like a police station…these guys were COPS, NCIS and I was being arrested. I was being charged with a violation of the military code of conduct. Another guy in the barracks accused me of stealing his transistor radio, but God strike me dead, I did not do what I was being charged with. And with that, I would stay in trouble for another seven weeks.

I now was placed in a "restriction barracks" and my freedom was held to a minimum. Needless to say, I was scared to death. I would meet with an assigned military defense counselor the next day and that's when the fun began. After reading the charges to me, he looked me straight into my eyes and asked, "why did you do this?" Like I said earlier, I had learned not to take much crap and I was not ready for any, so I politely told him in a very vocal tone "I did not do this!" He sat back in his chair, informed me that he was an officer in the US Navy and would not be talked to like that. OK, then don't accuse me of something I didn't do. I would also have meetings with the prosecutor and we had much the same conversations. This little circus went on almost daily for at least four weeks. Each time I would be asked the same questions and each time they got the same answer.

Of course when I had the opportunity to call home I did. I gave the whole story to my aunt and she knew I was not guilty. She immediately said she would talk to their friend, George, who was a retired Army Colonel and had headed court-martial boards during WWII. A time was scheduled for me to call him later, and that's when he gave me the trip around the track. Asking much of the same questions, I told him point blank that I did not do this and would NOT under any circumstances say that I did. He had known me since I was eight years old. He knew when I was BS'ing, and by my tone knew that I in fact did not do it. He advised me to call him back in a few days and after doing some research we would go from there.

I couldn't wait to call him back. I had no idea of what he was going to tell me and hoped that maybe he would change my luck. He questioned if the defense and prosecutor had changed their tactics. They had not! I was then told to hold to my stern commitment of "not guilty" and not to waiver no matter what threats would be placed before me. He assured me all would be good. Nice to hear but I was not convinced.

I was being court-martialed for something I did not do and if found guilty would spend 6-months in prison, demotion in rank, loss of pay, and God knows what else. The date was set and I was a week away from hell.

More trips to the legal department when one day my defense lawyer again asked me the same questions. In a very sullen tone I declared once again that I was "not guilty." He looked me in the eyes, leaned forward and said, "you're telling me the truth aren't you?" I couldn't respond. I was out of gas and the bus was coming to a halt. He told me to sit there and he left the room. About 20 minutes went by before he returned. We both then went to the prosecutor's office and again I was asked the same question. I damn near cried. I just said "no," the prosecutor looked at me and said "I believe you...everything will be taken care of," and he proceeded to fill me in with all the details of what was going to happen. All this crap was Greek to me but it sounded good.

I called George that night and filled him in on what had happened. He was overjoyed. My luck was turning around. I could feel the vice around the family jewels loosening. What was going to happen, George explained, was I would be charged in court, asked how I pled, would be cross-examined and the court would council. After the verdict I would be given sentence, then be led away. Any sentence given would receive a CA (Command Authority), which in my case would be overturned and I would go on about my business and no one would know. I trusted George but I was scared as hell.

Well my luck had not gotten better as someone didn't get the message. I was found guilty, sentenced to 6 months in the brig, and demoted with loss of pay. A marine guard escorted me out of the court room and led me to a jail cell. I sat in that cell for at least four hours while others were finding their fates. I wondered why I was not being released as I was told, but dared not ask. The cell filled up and around 1800 hrs (that's 6:00 at night) the marine came back, opened the jail and marched our asses out into the grinder and we headed off to the BRIG. My heart was pounding! What was going on? The gates at the San Diego brig opened and hell was waiting. Our heads were shaved, belongings went into a closet, issued prison uniforms and led to our cells. That was the worst night of my life.

If you get to sleep for two hours at a time you're lucky. The marines that run the brig love to give the sailors as much pain and torture as possible. I thought boot camp was a pain in the ass...hell, that was heaven and I didn't even know it. There are people watching all the new prisoners and after about four days, you are evaluated as to the type of prisoner you are. Were you trouble, an escape artist, gay, suicidal, or just another lost soul. I was herded into an office where a 1st Class Petty Officer began the interview. He offered me some coffee and a cigarette. WOW! A HUMAN! He asked me several questions that I just don't remember and when he was finished he asked if I had any questions. Oh brother, did he really just do that? "How the hell do I get out of here?" It was the only thing on my mind and I let him have it. For a second I thought the prison alarm system was going to be activated but he held his composure and asked "what the hell did I mean?" As fast as I could, I gave him my plea. Shocked, stunned, in disbelief, he asked me if I was for real and I assured him quickly I was, and told him the story. He jumped out of his chair and darted out the door, and in about two minutes I hear this screaming voice yelling "LEE, GET YOUR ASS IN MY OFFICE!"

It seems both George and my aunt were awaiting the phone call after the court-martial. When it did not come, they panicked and started making phone calls to George's contacts. Typical, no one had a clue as to what, where and how I disappeared. And to make matters worse, I was now listed as AWOL because I did not show up at the legal department as planned. This is what I call a classic government failure! My aunt had her congressman involved, a lawyer, and God knows who else trying to find me. There I was camped right under everyone's nose in the San Diego Brig. SOMEONE had not gotten the word and it fell on the Major's desk...and he was not a happy man.

So at double time, I headed to the Major's office. I stood before his desk at the tightest attention I could muster. He questioned my being, my everything, because I was causing him grief. I was causing him grief? Look ass-hole, I'm in this God-forsaken hell hole and you think you've got grief? He then informed me that I had five minutes to get my shit out of his closet and get my ass out of his BRIG…no problem Major…DONE! The gate opened up and there stood my defense counselor, white as a ghost with fright in his eyes. Someone had screwed up big time and there was going to be hell to pay. Just for the record, if that happened in today's legal world, I could be worth millions. I just wanted to go to my ship and forget the whole damn thing and hope everyone else would do the same.

Immediately we went to the legal department building. There I was honored like a king, a rock star and hero. I was offered coffee and an office with phone so I could call my family. Someone had called my aunt already but that didn't stop her tears when she heard my voice. My lawyer was as nervous as a cat trying to cover up shit on a tin roof. He was pushing the clerks to get the paper work finalized. A phone rang and when answered, it was handed to me. It was the CA, the base commander, and he was apologizing to me - ME - the lowest piece of shit on the planet. He explained that a mistake had been made and not to worry, there would be no hint of this on my record and there never was! It went away like a puff in the wind. Amazing how the government can make things go away! He did ask if there was anything I needed and I quickly said, "I need some money." All my records, including pay records, had been forwarded to the Cimarron and I had not a dime to my name. I then handed the phone off to the clerk and "emergency pay" was immediately ordered for me. Finally, we finished signing papers and I was free! I headed to the barn for a hot shower and into my "liberty" duds. The paymaster was next and I picked up $30 and out the gate I went into San Diego for some fresh air.

I relaxed for a few days with no duty, just acting like a tourist when finally my walking papers arrived; I was finally heading to Japan to board The Cimarron.

A whole gaggle of us boarded a plane and flew to a military base in the San Francisco area. After grabbing a bite to eat, we boarded an MSTS flight headed for Japan with stops in Honolulu, Wake Island and then Tachikawa Air Base in Japan.

We flew all night, arriving early in the morning at Hickam Field in Honolulu as the sun was rising. I was not much into history or reading at this age, but I did know what had happened on this field December 7, 1941. Standing on the tarmac and staring at the mountains, a voice behind me said "there," pointing in the direction of a mountain pass. "That's where the Japs flew through." He had been here and watched as they attacked. This guy, who was a Hawaiian, had survived the onslaught of that day. I was in total awe.

After a brief breakfast and a trip to the head to do our business and wash our faces, we boarded the plane. Next stop Wake Island, another significant island that movies were made of and history borne. Our stop was for re-fueling only and we were not allowed off the plane. The next stop was Japan and Tachikawa Air Base. We circled Mt. Fuji at dusk and the site was breathtaking.

After landing we boarded a bus that took us on what had to have been the road so honored in the song "40 miles of bad road." It was about a 40-mile trek with pot holes that could swallow basketballs. Anyone with fillings in their teeth needed a dentist after that ride.

Arriving at Yokosuka Naval Station, I was headed to yet another barn. It was late so I bedded down for a much-needed rest and was awake by 0600. I took a quick shower, went to chow hall, then to muster at 0800. After muster I was called to the office and informed they couldn't find my ship. COULDN'T FIND MY SHIP? THE SON OF A BITCH IS 850 FEET LONG AND YOU CAN'T FIND IT? That's the military for you. It's always hurry up and wait, and now they can't find my ship. It is a wonder how we ever won our independence. So "what now?" I asked. They would get back to me. It didn't take long and in about two hours I was called back and told I was headed to Subic Bay in the Philippines as The Cimarron had been moved to operate in the South China Sea. I would be boarding a flight the next day so be ready to depart at 0900. OK, see ya then!

At 0900, several of us got on a bus and headed back to where this mess began and another trip down the "40 miles of bad road." We boarded a C-137 and off we went. I am going to tell you flat out, this was not TWA. Guys went into battle on these things and how they managed is beyond me. This baby holds dozens of troops and equipment and I just prayed that we were NOT being issued parachutes for deployment over Subic Bay. It was hot, smelly, noisy as hell, and there was no beverage service! We landed in Okinawa where some got off and others got on, and we were quickly back in the air.

We arrived at Clark Air Force base late in the afternoon. I couldn't help but stare across the tarmac wondering which direction Bataan was and the path of the "Death March." The scene was breathtaking! Another bus ride down a road that was clearly designed by the idiots who created the one in Japan, only this one was in the jungle. We arrived at Subic Bay Naval Station after dark and, you got it, another new barn.

The Cimarron was at sea so I was stuck in the new barn for about a week doing what one always does when stuck in this situation. Go to muster at 0800 and get your daily assignment to keep you busy.

One day I was assigned to a gun crew! I politely explained that I was a radioman, not a gunners-mate and was told to get MY ASS IN THE TRUCK. Looks like I'm going to learn something new today. We were going to present a "5-gun" salute over the bay. The person being so honored was onboard a ship from some country I had never heard of and have not heard of since. Because an admiral was aboard, our government needed to honor him with a 5-gun salute. All cute and in our best white uniforms, one by one the shells were placed in the "battery" and fired. All I did was stand there and salute. After the final shell went off I had to inquire, "what in the hell were you aiming at?" I didn't see any explosions. "Blanks, you idiot" was the reply. Oh yea, that makes sense. See, I really did learn something that day. The next day I would be on my new home, the USS Cimarron.

In a port, ships are moored at piers or anchored. When several ships need to be moored on the same pier, they're placed side by side. Seniority then has its privileges. In this scenario, that means the rank of the Captain of the ship gets the best position, which means next to the pier and next to land. Confused? I know. The "Captain" of a ship most often is not a captain by rank. He is the Captain because he is the senior officer and in charge of that vessel.

In the Navy, a Captain is the equivalent to a Colonel in the other branches of service. More confusing, in the Navy, a Lieutenant is the same as a Captain in the other services. Keeping all that straight in boot camp was just one of our problems. The Captain of the Cimmaron was, in fact, Captain by rank, which normally would mean he would be moored next to the pier and just steps away from solid ground. That is convenience for him and his crew. Still confused?

When boarding a Navy vessel, one must salute the "ensign" or the flag, then salute the OD (Officer on Deck) and ask permission to board. Ok, you're on the first ship but you need to get to the next ship. So you pass through and now you need to proceed to the next vessel. Again you must salute the "ensign" and ask permission to board the next ship. These steps are repeated until you reach your destination. A pain for sure, and if the ship you need to reach is the fourth, well, you get it!

I needed to reach the fourth ship in line and I was toting that damn duffle again. Not only was the Cimarron the fourth ship in line, she (a ship is called "she") was on the furthest pier. The ranking systems made no sense at all. A high-ranking officer had the worst position in Subic Bay Naval Yard. Why?

When I finally reached the Cimarron I was greeted by the OD, a messenger and Petty Officer. Two of the three had black eyes. Hmmm, this must be a rough ship! I was led to my quarters, then off to the personnel office with my package of official papers. Next stop, was the Operations Officer's state room. This was going to be the officer whom I would work under.

This was not a good meeting! After knocking and being granted permission to enter, I was greeted by, "so you're the troublemaker we've been waiting for!" I dared not look behind me as surely he wasn't referring to me. All he knew about me was that I had a warrant from the San Diego Police Department for a parking ticket, had been court-martialed and was listed as AWOL. GOOD GOD, nobody got the WORD! After telling me that he would do everything in his power to get rid of my sorry ass, I was excused.

After that ordeal, I wasn't sure if I would be thrown overboard or hung from the yard-arm. Fortunately, I had little or no contact with him during the remainder of the cruise. Then off to the radio room to get acquainted and posted on a "watch list."

During these travels, I noted several black eyes or other maladies that bore the looks of a "gang" fight. I was getting worried as a few of the officers were also blessed with scars of battle.

It seems that during a refueling operation involving the aircraft carrier USS Essex and their Marine air wing, things got out of hand. The marines and sailors on the Essex were not pleased with Cimarron's service. During a refueling, words like, "we'll see you in Subic Bay" and other pleasantries were exchanged and tempers flared.

Here again, seniority is king, and any resupply vessel is in "control" regardless of the rank of the ship being resupplied. That meant the Cimarron was in charge and at this point the Captain was not happy with the way refueling was being handled on the Essex and ordered the "plug" pulled, spilling crude oil all over the deck of the Essex. Pulling the plug is an emergency measure that is controlled for safety reasons so that the two ships can separate quickly. That makes for one hell of a messy cleanup. Not nice! People get angry over little things like this and bad blood can happen...and did about a week later.

Upon arriving back in port after the refueling debacle, one of my fellow radiomen went into town and was discovered by a few of the marines who had to do the cleanup. Pay backs can be hell, but three to one is not fair.

After being taken to the hospital, repaired and sent back to the Cimarron, things apparently got out of control. Our executive officer, who had risen from the ranks of the enlisted and then became an officer, was a tough old bird and would not tolerate such nonsense.

A gathering of key people, a "dungaree party," was called. That's a good old-fashioned "ass kicking party." Yep, the exec took several of the enlisted and a few officers into town and started kicking some serious booty.

Well you can imagine the outcome of that! The first thing was the "Captain" of the Cimarron was put on the carpet for allowing this to happen. He had nothing to do with it, but with rank and privilege comes responsibilities. He was placed on probation and ordered to "Captain's Mast" those that were involved. Part of his punishment was losing mooring position for the duration of his deployment. The marines and sailors on the Essex also had punishments but I do not know what they were, as shortly after this little circus, she was sent on another mission and we never came in contact with them again.

The poor exec was passed over for rank and having been in the Navy for almost thirty years was asked to "retire." The battle was talked about for weeks but not in the Captain's presence.

The remainder of our assignment was spent refueling our fleet stationed off the coast of Vietnam (yes, we were there in '62), then returning to Subic Bay to refill the tanks and then back out to sea.

On one of these return trips we side-tracked to Hong Kong for some R & R. I had just passed my test for the rate of Seaman and having passed, was now a Radioman Seaman and with that came an $18 a month raise. I would have some extra spending money for the trip. The site was unbelievable, something I will never forget. One cannot envision the view unless you have been there, as pictures cannot do it justice. The bay waters are massive and they go for miles and miles in all directions. There must have been 10,000 vessels going in every possible direction.

Loaded with millions of gallons of fuel, we had to anchor way away from the mass of humanity called Hong Kong. It took 45 minutes by "liberty boat" to get to shore and was not a smooth ride as white caps are common in that bay.

Not keeping a log at this time, I do not remember how long we spent in Hong Kong but I had liberty on four occasions. I had a suit made, learned how to eat with chop sticks, explored the piers where tens of thousands of people were born, lived and died, had my first rickshaw ride, and discovered one of my favorite things, real "fried rice." Not sure I want to know what was in it but with a few beers, it tasted fantastic. And of course, I met a few of the local girls. Here I was 19 and halfway around the world. I joined the Navy to see the world and it was really happening.

We began our return to the states in May with a stop in Guam to off-load some fuel before heading to Pearl Harbor. One of my buddies from high school had become an electronics technician (ET) and was stationed at the Guam Radar Station. I actually got permission for a 48-hour liberty, made arrangements for transport to the other side of the island, and met with Bob to explore island life.

Bob was a true character with many talents, one of which was magic. Most islanders freak out with such nonsense except for the witch-doctors and some of the elders. Most of the villagers around the base thought of him as some sort of God-like creature. He loved it and who wouldn't, as it gave him the insight that not many get to see. He would do magic shows for many of the village childrens' birthday parties or other such events, for free, which really placed him on a pedestal. That night, thanks to Bob, we attended a Guamanian wedding, which was like nothing I have seen since. What a feast and celebration. I kinda' remember most of it, I think, as the next thing I remember was waking up in his barn. The visit was short, but so nice to see someone I grew up with, especially after what I had been through these past few months.

Leaving Guam, all hands were preparing the ship for "dry dock." The major thing happening was cleaning the storage "cells" that held the fuel.

The inner hull is designed much like a honey-comb and the thick crude oil builds up on those bulkheads (walls). It has to be scraped and removed periodically as it adds unwanted weight to the ship and reduces its capacity. This is not a pleasant job and I somehow, the bad boy that I was, got out of having to take my turn in the HOLE. Next stop Pearl!

Our stay was short in Pearl Harbor but we spent a little time exploring the sites before heading to our home port in Long Beach, California. The visit was so short I hardly remember even being there.

Arriving in Long Beach, we docked where ships go for dry-docking and refurbishing. This tends to be messy, dirty and a long way to go just to leave the base. Little did I know my time aboard the Cimarron was coming to an end.

Shortly after we arrived in Long Beach, the dreaded letter arrived from my belle at home. It was the Dear John letter all servicemen hate to receive. She had to say goodbye as she couldn't stand not to know where I was or what was going to happen to me. I knew it was coming but I struggled with it for some time and it had a profound effect on me for many months to come. I no longer wanted to be so close to someone that they could break my heart.

Sometime in mid July of '62, I was called to the Operations Officer's state room. Oh here we go again. Entering, I was greeted with "I told you I would get rid of your ASS! You're going to Staten Island"...at least that is what I remembered hearing. At first I felt joy and excitement...the Big Apple! Fun City! Lots of chicks! What he really said was, "You're going to the Staten Island and you're going to the South Pole!" The words South Pole entered my pea-sized brain and I froze (I love puns). I had been a model sailor, caused him no grief, did my job, and learned how to be a sea-going radioman, and this guy was on my ass. I wanted to give him a nasty reply, but I held my tongue. I left his state room and headed to the personnel office to get my orders and travel pay, and I said good-by to my new-found friends. I packed that damn duffle, again, and left the ship. I had six days to get to Seattle and money (per-diem) to get there. Checking flights and the bus schedule, I decided the bus was much cheaper and I would have extra spending money when I reached Seattle.

Boarding that Greyhound, I had no idea just how long of a bus ride this would be. I had pictured this scenic drive up the coast with a few stops at a couple of watering holes. No, this baby went inland and stopped at every hole-in-the-wall town from Long Beach to Seattle. I swore I would NEVER ride a bus again. I was on that damn bus for three days. With some stops lasting up to an hour, there was time to catch a bite to eat and take a sink bath. I was ready for the comforts of a shower.

Once we reached the border of Washington, I began to get excited. The scenery was much better and the trip was getting shorter. Being 19 and living in a cloud, I was not aware that the 1962 World's Fair was opening in Seattle. What memories awaited I was not prepared for. As we entered the south side of Seattle, the view of Puget Sound appeared. This would be my new home for the next two and a half years.

The top country hits of the time: Don't go near the Indians, I've been Everywhere, Crazy (Willie Nelson). The Top 40 hits of the time: I Can't Stop Loving You, Let's Dance, Green Onions, Do You Love Me?.

CHAPTER 5

THE USS STATEN ISLAND

As we got closer to downtown Seattle, the bus driver was telling us about the World's Fair and to look out towards the sound. There it was, the HMS Bounty, the one used in the Marlon Brando movie "Mutiny on the Bounty." It had been built half-scale for the movie and was one of the ships used in the opening ceremonies of the World's Fair. Of course, I had no camera in hand and my little Brownie would not have done the justice needed to capture the moment. Little did I know that in less than a year, I would be where the real HMS Bounty had been, Drakes Passage, in a storm.

The bus arrived at the depot in downtown Seattle. I couldn't get off fast enough, and headed to the YMCA two blocks away. I rented a locker and headed to the showers. I think I stayed in there for at least 30 minutes and it almost felt as good as home. The "Y" in downtown Seattle was a busy place. There were many rooms to rent and they offered a pool, pin-ball machines, pool tables, and a great dance floor and band stand that drew many fine chicks on Friday and Saturday nights.

All fresh after my great shower and dressed for my duties, I hailed a cab and off to Pier 91 to board the USS Staten Island (AGB-5). As we pulled up to her, I thought what a funny looking mess she was. Not extremely long (269'), a bit wide (63'), a 5-inch gun mount forward, a flight deck aft, and at over 6,000 tons she sat fully loaded at a draft of nearly 25 feet. I paid the driver, grabbed that damn duffle and boarded my new home. This was a very different experience than that of the Cimarron, and I was immediately taken to the radio room and greeted with open arms. After introductions, I was led to our compartment, dropped the duffle, and went one deck below to the personnel office and presented them with my paperwork. I was two days early but there was a warm bed and three square meals that cost me nothing, and I wanted to get going.

The Staten Island was a "Wind" class ice breaker. Her keel was laid in 1942 and finished in 1944 at which time she was assigned to the USSR as lend-leased material. The Russians named her "Severny Veter" (meaning Northwind) and operated in the Northern Sea. She was returned to the United States (Boston) in 1951 and commissioned in the US Navy. In 1955, her homeport was transferred to Seattle, Washington.

Well designed for work in ice, her bow was sloped, which enabled her to ride up on the ice. She was propelled by two 20-ton propellers and driven by six diesel engines that produced 10,000 horsepower that allowed her to crush up to 10 feet thick ice with her weight. The rounded hull helped prevent her from being crushed as ice flows move in. In open water she is capable of reaching speeds of up to 15 knots. The specially designed anti-roll tanks helped to make her stable in open water. Of course that was what the designers and engineers claimed but I'm here to tell you for her to reach 15 knots, nitro would have to fuel the engines and a downhill path employed. Without those anti-roll tanks, it would have been a disaster just to leave port. Icebreakers were not for open water.

The ship was preparing for a long cruise that would find us leaving Seattle in the middle of September and coming back mid to late March if we were lucky. At this point, I was totally in the dark about what we are going to do but I knew that info would come soon enough. It seemed everyone was busy with something, busier than norm, like we were going to leave in the morning. The crew turns over about 40-50% after each long cruise and that was the case with the Staten Island. I was just one of many new faces;

some were already aboard with more to follow before we departed. Much would change before then. Meanwhile, I had plenty of time to explore Seattle and the World's Fair.

My first trip to the Fair was hard to describe. I had no idea what to expect. There was this space-like monorail that went from the Fair to downtown Seattle, futuristic buildings that sent my architecture brain into swirls, fountains and water-pools, and of course the Space Needle. It stood magnificently with its spiral top and towered over the city and the sound. All these things are still used and enjoyed today. I would be back here many times to enjoy and photograph it.

The drinking age was 21 in Washington, and that was going to be a bummer for awhile, but it wouldn't take long to solve that problem. The area on the west side of downtown Seattle was a mass of piers, markets, some sleazy bars as well as some very cool jazz bars, which I would enjoy when I got older. The hub of downtown was filled with fine stores featuring everything from fine furs to blue jeans, a few great book stores, restaurants, and nightclubs. It was where people went to shop and have a good time. Seattle was not a destination like it is today, and the residents didn't mind that at all; it was their private oasis. The University of Washington and surrounding area is one of the finest places in America. Coffee shops, boutiques, bars, book stores, and fine-looking women adorned the streets. The campus is located on Lake Washington and the view is breathtaking. The lake is connected to Puget Sound via a lock system so you may see 200-foot yachts cruising or just a small sailboat. With Mt Rainier to the southeast, I stood in awe of God's creation. I would enjoy this city and call it home for many months to come, and I was ready to give it a ride.

Each day new shipmates would arrive and soon all the new radiomen would be onboard and getting to know one another. All sailors seem to go by their last names or nicknames, some of which they came with or were given once they arrived depending on their personality or habits. I was simply Lee. The other newbies were RB, Big Don, and Fred. We were all about the same age and with the same amount of experience. Our head radioman was a Chief Petty Officer, a career sailor, known as Shakey for obvious reasons.

If you looked up the word "wimp" in your Funk & Wagnalls, you would see Shakey's face. The new ETs (electronic technicians) were EJ and Gipe, and a new radarman became known as Jump.

RB, Big Don and I would end up good friends and spend a long time together on this vessel. The older radiomen were a mixed bag. There was Frenchie from Kansas. He knew as much about being in a radio shack as I know about being in the boiler room...NOTHING. Two guys from Arkansas - Freddie and Widener, and a good ole boy from Oklahoma. Chuckles was his handle and that says it all. Based on experience, we all would be put together to form watch groups before we sailed but for now us newbies did all the crap duty.

One thing that had to happen in the radio room was to get more radio receivers. These were used for dialing in frequencies to copy incoming and outgoing voice and Morse-code messages. The radio room looked complete to me, but what the hell did I know? It seems that where we were going, we could not take certain "classified" equipment due to treaties with "rite of passage" clauses. To put it in simple words, the Navy did not want the Russians to see what we had. We were going to use WWII and Korean War vintage equipment in the radio room. This should be good. Bottom line, we were going to become experts at sending Morse code but first we needed the equipment.

Bremerton, Washington is across Puget Sound and there is a huge "moth-ball fleet" (decommissioned ships), which was the perfect place to pick up the needed equipment. Big Don and I volunteered and, with no one objecting, we were on a mission.

With proper paperwork and the keys to the ship's van, we were off to catch the ferry to Bremerton. We had no idea what we were to bring back; that was in the paperwork, and all we knew was the base was across the sound. One would have to be blind not to find the damn thing...it's larger than life and filled with hundreds of decaying ships. The MPs took us to where we needed to go, walking us down a massive pier with ships of every size surrounding us. We soon met the sailor who was going to lead us to our treasures.

When you look at a ship from the side, you can just about judge the size; even at an angle, it's not too difficult. But looking down the bow, it's a bit of a challenge. As we reached the home of our new treasures, I was looking down this bow and thinking "holy crap - this boat is huge." We turned to go to mid-ship where we would board this behemoth when I saw the 63. OMG! It's the Missouri, BB-63. Both Big Don and I were in awe. Her size was unreal and we were about to board this beauty. Once aboard, the guy showed us around a little. When the Missouri was recommissioned in 1986, I can remember the lump I had in my throat knowing I had been aboard her.

We then went to the main radio room. Looking at the paper work, he motioned to a rack of receivers and said "take those." Full of dust from years of non-use, we unhooked them, put them on a cart and headed out of the ship into the van.

These receivers needed new tubes and some adjusting but they were built like tanks and served us well for months to come. I bet they would still work today...Hell, they were made in America!

Supplies kept coming on board and were lowered into the bowels of the ship. I had no idea those were the supplies we'd be using in the event we got stuck in the ice and had to "winter over." WINTER OVER! I didn't join to winter in Antarctica. I wanted hula skirts and Mai Tai's. More supplies would come aboard when we got to San Diego and then Pearl Harbor, and yet more before we left New Zealand to head into the ice. We were in for one helluva journey!

Time was short as we would leave Seattle mid September, so we had to get to know one another. Big Don and I were like two peas in a pod and hit it off right away. We decided to hit the beach and see what we could find in Seattle. The downtown offered something for just about every walk of life. What we were interested in was down by the docks or the east end of Pike. That's where the bars were that fit our style. We were in need of finding someone who would sell us a beer. Now, put two sailors with a mission like that loose in Seattle, something is going to happen.

After about four failures, being carded at each, we hit gold...an old bar just east of Pike and 8th Ave, run by what looked like nice grandparents. They loved servicemen and we fit the mold. We had found our home away from home. There was one small problem though as "Smitty's Bar" was across the street and was a well known hang out and favorite to get anything you wanted to drink, dance with, well, you get the point. Being such a place, the cops and SPs (Shore Patrol) were there often, and many times they would check out other locations for problems…and we were problems because we were underage.

After a few visits, and we visited often, the old couple took us under their wings and treated us as family. They were shocked to find out we were headed to Antarctica and wanted to make sure we were filled to the gullet with beer any time we felt the need...which was almost daily.

When we went to their tavern, they always made sure we sat at the far end of the bar as those seats were closest to the storage room. The old lady had a mirror on the wall that allowed her to view the street to the west and could see anyone (cops or SPs) walking up. On at least two occasions, she saved our asses and shoved us into the storage room and locked the door. We had found true love. On the bar were jars of pickled eggs and jerky. Big Don and I fell in love with these snacks and couldn't get enough. On our last visit prior to sailing south, they presented us with full jars of both. We loved those people; they were like folks from home.

Big Don always found some extra energy after about four or five beers. It was called courage and he had this profound need to kick someone's ass. Now this can only lead to problems and as we got closer to our departure date, we had an incident that I was unable to stop. That night, after being served more than our fair share, Big Don went into another rant. As we walked down Pike towards the docks, he would challenge any male that approached. Most laughed, the rest just walked away. Now he's pissed. Nobody was cooperating, and now he had another urge...he had to pee. Near the docks was an old flop house owned by a Chinaman, with a flight of stairs leading up to the desk. Now this was a dive for sure but all these joints had hallway bathrooms. Up we went and the old Chinaman went nuts. In broken English he tried his best to stop us and of course failed. Standing at the urinal, relieving himself of all the beer he had consumed, Big Don began smashing the walls with his fists. Oops! Now we have a hole in the wall, then two, then three, and the Chinaman was now speaking to us in his native tongue and I'm sure he was calling us bad things. He had called the cops and of course they arrived before we had the chance to leave. We were each receiving our first ride in a paddy wagon. The cops did convince the old Chinaman to take cash for the repairs in lieu of seeking legal action. Quickly paying, we were then escorted into the rear of the paddy wagon and off to the police station.

These cops could not stop laughing. They had had many trips to this flop house and there was no love lost between either party; however, they did have to call the SP's and they showed up quickly. Knowing that we're heading to Antarctica in a very short time, they just took us back to the Staten Island and informed the OD (officer of the deck) that we had just been over-served. We really got lucky that night.

The next day, again getting ready to head south, much work still needed to be done. A new antenna needed to be installed to support those new receivers. You guessed it, Big Don and I got the job. It's called pay-back. The main mast above the bridge was where this damn thing needed to be attached. It needed to be pulled up to the top to make that happen. With heads pounding from the action the night before, we slowly climbed up the ladder towards the "crows-nest." The only thing that still bothers me is why we didn't fall and bust our asses! After returning to the safety of the deck, we had forgotten our headaches; amazing what fright can do for such maladies.

September 22, 1962. Finally, it seemed we were ready. All that remained was the POMP prior to sailing. It seems the Navy likes POMP - bands, mothers, dads, wives, children and, of course, the BRASS. The big send off! Banners waving and most all family members crying. I never did get that; don't think I ever will. Now the big question for most of us was what the hell faces us next? We pulled away from Pier 91 and headed west down

Puget Sound. It was 125 miles to the ocean and the sun would be setting before we would be on the high seas.

This would end up being one long boat ride, well over 25,000 nautical miles by the time we returned to Pier 91. It was a trip I will never forget.

The top country hits of the time: She Still Thinks I Care, PT 109, Adios Amigo. The Top 40 hits of the time: Sheila, Breaking Up is Hard To Do, Big Girls Don't Cry, Peppermint Twist.

CHAPTER 6

OPERATION DEEP FREEZE 63

September 22, 1962, 0800 hours, Operation Deep Freeze 63 began for the USS Staten Island and her crew. After all the POMP, the ship prepared for departure with our first stop in San Diego. We officially got underway at 0900. The trip out Puget Sound to the Pacific Ocean is a long one as Seattle is about 130 miles by land to reach the ocean and by water it's a few more nautical miles. Plodding along at 12 to 13 knots, it will be sunset before we feel the waves of the massive, never-ending ocean.

The trip to San Diego was about as normal as could be with seas fairly calm, with overcast and cloudy skies most of the way. Normal routine for all of us with many drills, testing of equipment, and just getting into the groove of what would be a very long journey covering many thousands of miles.

Nearing San Diego on the 26th, we held flight quarters and received our two helicopters and flight crews. They would serve us well in the months to come. We arrived late and finally tied up at 1700. Big Don and I hit the beach but found nothing exciting so we headed back to the ship early. On the 27th, liberty call began at 1300 and we hit the beach again. We fooled around for a few hours, then he left to meet his parents who came to visit from Riverside, California, his hometown. I later met Stephanie and her roommate, both students at San Diego State, and we had dinner and shared old memories. Stephanie was one of my old belle's best friends and classmate. It was fun as well as sad to talk about home. The next time we would see each other would be in 1965, and oh how I would change by then.

We were scheduled to depart for Pearl on the 28th, but one of our generators was found to be nonfunctioning on our trip from Seattle and could not be fixed correctly so a replacement had to be made. We ended up with two more days in San Diego and I stayed onboard, as I could save some money and I had seen enough of this city for now.

We departed at 0900 on the 30th, headed to Pearl, and soon settled into our routine. In the radio room our watch schedules were in three shifts, day watch, eve watch and mid watch. For the record, all other shipboard watches are 4 hours in length. Each watch had two men on duty and they would rotate these shifts as long as we were at sea. This only required 6 men and we had 10 radiomen plus Shakey, the chief. Normally, the lower-rated guys would stand the shift watches while the senior guys had other clerical jobs or just sat around on their asses like our friend, Frenchie. The day watch began after breakfast and ended at dinner, eve was dinner until midnight, and the mid was midnight until breakfast. It takes awhile to get into the groove and we had lots of time ahead of us. Being the rookies in the radio room, we were most always relieved of our duties during the day watch by the senior guys so we could do the grunt work. But when push came to shove and things got serious, rank didn't mean that much and that's where RB and I came in. He and I were clearly the best key operators. It's not bragging when it's the truth. Not one of the other radioman, even the Chief, could put a match to us on the key. This fact would come to light the following year in the Arctic during encounters with the Russians.

On the 3rd of October, I had 21 outgoing messages waiting for me when I arrived on watch. That was one hell of a load, but as usual they were sent, accepted and filed. On the 4th, my reputation, good or bad, began as LTJG Stevans accused me of leaving water running (a major no-no at sea as fresh water is precious). Accused is the operative word here as I had and still have no idea what and where that happened and he would never explain it to me. But I was given a 4 hour watch over an evaporator (in my free time of course), like someone or something was going to walk off with it? Really stupid shit! This guy would be a giant pain in my ass in the months to come.

The 5th of October was yet another learning session as Widener, Gipe and I were awarded the privilege to holy-stone the stack deck. Ice Breakers have wooden decks and they get dirty. Well some old salt in the olden days of wooden ships figured out you could clean them with a fricken' stone. This porous stone had a notch in the middle where a broom handle was placed for easy scrubbing. Basically you're sanding the deck. God, I'm getting really talented. Mr. Holy Stone and I would share special moments many times again.

For the next three days, the whole ship went nuts, cleaning, scrubbing, fixing and repairing all for the "big" inspection when we arrived in Pearl. I'm not quite sure why this happens; it must be an ego thing for Admirals and other top brass. Would you enjoy inspecting a head or a scullery? These guys must not have much to do. Preparing for such events means no one is exempt; 2nd and even 1st class Petty Officers grab paint brushes or mops or rags or whatever to prepare for the "special occasion."

October 9th. We pulled into Pearl and for a US sailor, it puts a lump in your throat every time you enter this channel. We all have seen the pictures of the destruction and one cannot forget those who lost their lives that day. The 21st anniversary of that tragedy was just three months away.

After mooring and all the hoopla involved, the BIG inspection began. What a total farce as it lasted all of ten minutes. We busted our asses for a ten-minute inspection; you gotta' love the military way. Inspection done, Big Don and I made a burn run. A burn run is simply destroying radio room trash beyond recognition. Everything, no matter if it's personal letters or whatever, if it is thrown in the trash it gets burned. At Pearl they had this monstrous incinerator that would melt a car into BB's in seconds, so you can imagine what would happen to a big paper bag filled with papers. Poof! Gone! Back aboard the Staten Island, we spent the rest of the day doing sailor things, anticipating our first visit to this place laden with tiki bars, hula skirts and Mai Tai's.

At some point after joining the Navy, I somehow got interested in reading. Not sure how that happened but I always had a paperback in the works. It was most always fiction, but reading is educational no matter what. I had started reading Richard Prather's "Shell Scott" mystery/murder novels, and when Big Don and I first met, I discovered that he, too, was reading them. The character Scott was an ex-marine turned private eye from LA, and his favorite watering hole in the world was the "Skull and Bones" in none other than Waikiki. His favorite drink…shots of cognac, so we just had to give that a try.

After evening chow, we hit the beach in search of the "Skull & Bones" and it didn't take us long to find it. Located in a passageway off the main drag among several shops, we found our sought-after treasure. In we go, sashay up to the bar and order shots of cognac. Then those hated words: "Let's see those IDs." DAMN! Foiled again! The drinking age in Hawaii at that time was 20; surely he would let me go as I would turn 20 in 19 days. No way in hell that was going to happen as the threat of him losing his license was 100% if caught. And the bars, military personnel and civilians all feared the HASP (Hawaiian Armed Services Police) and the local police. Big Don had turned 20 in early September so he had his shot as I waited outside. He said it tasted like crap, so I had saved some money. We spent a little time walking around before we headed back to the ship.

In Pearl, more secret equipment was taken off and we began operating in CW (Morse Code) and teletype 100%. We really were going back in time now and all those hours spent practicing Morse code was going to pay off. Widener, Fred and I hit the beach but accomplished nothing, so we went back to the ship to get ready for tomorrow's activities. We are heading south.

October 11$^{th.}$ We took on AvGas for the helo's (helicopters) at the fuel depot and then departed at 1030 hours in route to Port Lyttleton, New Zealand. The weather was tropical and it was hard to imagine that in a very short time we would be in freezing weather.

October 12th. A change of plans abruptly came to us, and we altered course and were now on our way to Pago Pago. It seems that some sort of survey crew was working on one of the deserted islands in the chain and improperly anchored their boat. High tide came, the boat rose with the tide as did the anchor and Yep, it drifted away leaving them stranded. So off we go to save their asses. The next few days were just normal days at sea but everyone was awaiting the big "ceremony."

Today, October 15th was far from a normal day at sea. It was Pollywog Day, the calm before the storm. A Pollywog (that would be me) is an individual who has never crossed the International Date Line, a.k.a. equator. After crossing and being initiated, you become a Shellback and you will be a Shellback forever. It was our day to dress up like pirates and do some crazy things. Since leaving Pearl, all of the garbage from the mess hall had mysteriously disappeared. So a posse was formed and we went on a mission to find it and destroy it before it was used in tomorrow's charades. There are not many places one can hide 30-gallon trash cans filled with garbage, but sailors are sailors and strange things can happen. The emergency radio room was located two decks below the flight deck and no one ever goes in there. Quick like a bunny, I hopped back to the main radio room and slyly got the key and returned. WALA! We found two garbage cans full of garbage. After dark it was taken to the fan-tail (aft) and down the garbage chute it went. We were thrilled but discovered the next day that that was a bad mistake.

I had the mid watch so I was going to be dragging ass for a few days. Today the 16th of October, all Pollywogs were greeted with uncooked beans, water and coffee for breakfast while the Shellbacks devoured steak & eggs. Our dress for the day was simply flip-flops, t-shirts and dungaree pants, and at 0800 all Polywogs were to muster at the rails on port side (left) on hands and knees, asses in the air, and facing the ocean. The ship came dead-in-the-water, the ensign lowered, and a jolly roger was hoisted. King Neptune was now in command...oh shit! We're in trouble!

Fire hose comes in different sizes and depending on the need, 2, 4 or 6-inch hose is used. Old hose is thrown away. Well, some of it is saved for such events. Four-inch hose cut into lengths of about 24" to 36" makes a perfect whipping tool. You can picture what one's ass might look like after being smacked dozens of times.

As soon as the Jolly Roger was hoisted, all hell broke loose. It sounded like the attack at the Little Big Horn. Whooping and hollering and all dressed up like the finest pirates on the seas, they came running down the decks and choosing asses to smack. The first smack moved you forward a few inches but now you were ready for the next one and the next one. If you dared try to look at your assailant, you were in for much more so it was best to keep your eyes forward. After each smack they would ask you "WHAT ARE YOU?" and you better say a Polywog or the next smack would be quick. This went on for several minutes but then the ship's whistle blew and we were herded on hands and knees to the starboard side (right). One by one, we were taken to the "Kings" Court. There, in all their drag, were the King, his Queen, their baby, barber, judge, executioner, and a variety of other talented servants with their torture devices waiting.

It was getting warm and the sun was up bearing down, getting many to the point of dehydration. Being whipped like a dog with instruments of mass destruction takes the starch right out of you and the only thing on your mind is water.

Once your turn comes around, you crawl to the feet of the King & Queen and at that point a "court servant" reads the charges against you. Most are obscure and comical but some, like mine, were more on the truth side. I was charged with destroying the King's garbage....oops, here it comes. Looking at the Queen, she gave me the "thumbs down" and I was dragged on my hands and knees to the judge for my sentence. "Three swats by the executioner" and with that my already sore ass was smacked three times with what looked like a six foot 1 x 4. I'm talking sting here and I still had a long way to go. Next, the barber. Now after about an hour on your hands and knees, you climb into the barber chair and large chunks of your beautiful locks are randomly removed. The visit to the King and Queen's baby was vile. This character is always the heaviest, fattest sailor who has reached the pinnacle of Shellback. Dressed in a make-shift diaper, sitting in a chair, you're brought up to him and told to kiss his belly. That would be fowl enough by itself but a concoction of hot sauce, cumin, mustard, and God knows what else is put on his belly and you had damn well better give the best set of lips you can produce.

While all of this is going on, you are constantly getting smacked in the ass and asked "what are you?" I bet at least a hundred times during this whole process, and the worst was yet to come. By this time we had crawled our way towards the bow and I could see what appeared to be an above-ground swimming pool, and I dared not think about what that was for. To the left of the pool was a tube of canvas and I could see guys going in, crawling through and coming out the other end near the pool where they were promptly thrown in. Some of these poor slobs were pale; others were nearly green.

Feeling weak from lack of water and food and being scorched by the hot sun did not make the next step any easier. Remember those 30-gallon cans full of garbage? You guessed it! In the tunnel, cooking in the hot sun, I was next to crawl through. Flashes of escape passed my mind but I didn't want them to get the idea they could beat me at this game so I dove into the tunnel, held my breath, and slithered to the end. Then the do-over came, and back into the tunnel once again. After the second voyage in the tunnel, I was quickly picked up and thrown into the pool. After what we had been put through, it actually was relieving. Now, what hair I had left, was being grabbed and I was dunked again and again. After each dunk in, I was asked "WHAT ARE YOU?" There is only one answer to this question so the response is "POLYWOG." Wrong, back into the water and held for about 15-seconds then again "WHAT ARE YOU?" For me it took three dunks when finally the light went on. "SHELLBACK!" I finally, after over four hours of torture, reached the IMPERIVM NEPTVNI REGIS, The realm of Neptune.

Sore, thirsty, sun-burned, and hungry as hell, I needed a shower first. After a cool soak, it was to the chow hall where our "Steak & Eggs" were served with cold glasses of milk, cold water, and a good cup of coffee.

After everyone was done, the Jolly Roger came down, the Ensign was raised, our Captain took control of his ship, and we were again off to

New Zealand. My ass was bruised for about a week but some needed a trip to see the Doc. I lost count as to how many swats I had endured but those who had made enemies with the wrong people prior to this day paid a bigger price. Doing the mid watch from 0001 hours 'til 0730, then going through the charades, I now had to do the eve watch from 1750 till 0000; when will I ever catch up on some shut-eye?! I now could look forward to being on the other end, which unfortunately never happened. I crossed the equator only one other time and that was by air on a trip to Buenos Aires in 1973, and they don't celebrate aboard civilian airplanes. BUMMER!

Still en route to our rescue mission, we'll soon find ourselves off the American Samoan Islands. Early on the 19th, Flight Ops began and the Huey took off to pick up the surveyors and transport them to Pago Pago. Mission accomplished, we kept heading south.

The weather is gradually changing to cooler temps and the seas are not as smooth. We still had eight more days to go before reaching New Zealand and nothing in between but water.

With several boring days ahead, the Captain and his cronies came up with a plan and that's not ever good. Keep the swabs alert, create action, something to keep their minds sharp. Me, I'm thinking these three B's would work: broads, booze and BBQ. So every day we practiced emergencies and that calls for GQ, battle stations and all that crap. Now, at 1400 hours it's not so bad, but what's with this nonsense at 0300? That's the middle of the night! Coupled with the GQ's, we had inspections, both compartmental and personal. On the 25th, we crossed the Date Zone and we lost a day... it was a fricken' do-over, and that sucks!

Over the intercom came the speech by the executive officer regarding our little visit to New Zealand. This should be good! Be on your best behavior (sure we will), always and I mean always use condoms (yea, ok) and those growing beards we were told to shave as it might cause trouble (to this day, I have NEVER heard of a beard causing trouble). Beards may be grown again after we leave New Zealand...typical Navy Bull Shit!

Global news is not good and things are beginning to get serious. Many who were on the verge of getting out would be extended, and with the Russians and Cubans stirring the pot, no telling what might happen. We should be ok; who wants to fight a war in the South Pole?

On the early morning of the 27th, we could see land in the distance. We were hours away from liberty and the anticipation was explosive. As we neared, the water color was almost emerald and the mountain countrysides were turning green. Remember it's their spring on this side of the world. Folks at home are getting ready for snow and the natives here are getting ready to skinny-dip. Up the inlet we slowly navigated toward Port Lyttleton, our new home away from home. Finally, the pier was in site and all filled with people, supplies and mail. Mail is the life blood of all servicemen and they will deal with that first, above all others. Our official time of arrival was 1337; I had 38 on the anchor-pool so I won a hundred bucks…yipee, we're gonna have some fun tonight! There were pools for everything and it kept everyone excited. There would be several before we got back to Seattle. Being junior in the radio room, Fred and I naturally got the first watch shift. My Luck!

I couldn't believe the chicks on the pier, all waiting for a sailor to say "hellooooo" and I would miss out on that action, well, at least for tonight. Liberty was called around 1500 hours and the herd of rabbits left the ship, stumbling all the way down the ramp, trying to be first at reaching the chicks.

At midnight I turned 20 and had no place to go. Back in the day, liberty ended at 0100 hours while in foreign ports, so around midnight many began returning. Some being carried, some dragged, some covered with lip-stick and all having stories. Widner and Chuckles were good buddies and later took me under their wings, but this night, knowing it was my birthday, they smuggled a quart of New Zealand Ale aboard so I could have a little night-cap. God I loved them! A tad bitter for my liking but it was "free" and along with "cold and frequent," was and always has been my favorite brand. Tonight would be my turn so after the ale I headed to bed to rest for tomorrow's action.

The Top 40 hits of the time: The Wanderer, Roses are Red, Sherry

CHAPTER 7

OUR VISIT TO NEW ZEALAND

Port Lyttleton is a small seaport serving Christchurch and surrounding countryside. There were three ways to get to Christchurch from this small sea port; rail, vehicle, or walking. The distance by road was about 7-1/2 miles and took about 25 minutes to reach downtown Christchurch. There were cabbies everywhere so quick access to come and go was at your hands almost 24 hours a day. Big Don and I got to know two cabbies who were good ole' blokes and we shared many laughs together during our visits in New Zealand. One was very small in stature; the other looked like a sumo wrestler who needed to go on a serious diet. We never could figure out how in the hell he fit into those funny-looking little English cars. We would become regulars with these two cabbies and would see them again on our next visit.

Because of what was ahead of us, the Captain relaxed the noose a bit and let liberty be called daily at 1300 and that would give us 10 hours of balls-out freedom. He had months to squeeze the noose later and he knew we needed this brief respite of freedom to gain some strength.

At the end of the pier was an old-fashioned English pub that looked like it belonged in the countryside of jolly ole' England. It was at this pub that we could catch a cab, but a quick ale before the ride was always in order.

Inside was as bland as bland could be. A few beer/ale signs were hanging and of course dart boards everywhere, but it was dimly lit and very drab. The bar itself was a large square 10 to 12 feet on each side. Now, this is a pub and that means beer or ale only, so we sashayed up to the bar and ordered brews. This bloke grabbed two large mugs, put them on the bar, reached down and pulled up what looked like a garden hose and poured us our brews. These hoses, and there were several, went into the basement and attached to the kegs. The ale was cellar temperature but tasty. At 1800 hours a Bobbie would walk into these pubs, and that was the end of drinking. That's right, 6:00 p.m. in real time, the pubs close. There are always solutions to these types of problems and it wouldn't take us long to find out how to solve this one.

It was the 29th of October, I was now 20, and I couldn't wait to see what was doing. Widener, Chuckles, Frenchie, Fred and Big Don had been in town the day before and suggested that the cheapest place to grab some beers was at the New Zealand's Air Force EM Club so that's where we all ended up, and after several hours we were now drunk as…are you ready? ...sailors! Frenchie was like rubber, totally wasted, so the rest of us had to haul his sorry ass back to the ship and throw him in the sack.

The next day and all refreshed, Big Don and I hit the beach. After a few brews at the local pub we caught a cab with one of our new-found buddies and instructed him to take us where the action was. Knowing full well we weren't looking for a boutique, he dropped us at local hot spot, a "supper club." Ah, we've already found the solution. We paid the cabbie and he said he'd keep an eye out for us while in port. These guys were really becoming our friends and keepers.

Once inside, we knew this was a "hot spot" for sure. Nice dance floor, huge bar and lots of tables. It was about 1600 hours and the place was quiet. A few other guys from the ship, a few old chicks (they were probably in their 40s), and two bartenders were getting ready for when the work day ended. We sat at the bar, ordered our brews and waited. The wait was instant. The working civilians started pouring in, and the chicks were gorgeous and looking for someone to buy them a drink. RIGHT HERE DARLING!

Tonight was my lucky night. Chris and her girlfriend walked right up to us and invited us to a table. Bingo! The ride is in motion. After a few drinks and tons of bull shit, the girls asked if we wanted to head to their place... are you shitting me? You betcha.

These gals had jobs and had to be at work early the next day and just wanted to get to know us. We sat, drank some coffee and exchanged our life stories. It looked like we had found true love. They told us to call them the next day and we would make further plans. We called a cab and headed back to the ship, arriving around 2300. I dreamt of Chris all night long; she was attractive, educated and funny as hell. Big Don was also excited, which I could tell by his nose. He had this habit of rubbing his nose when he got excited or upset, and it was as red as a beet.

I called Chris on the morning of the 30th and she invited me to her place for the evening. Little known to me, Emma had tracked Big Don down and they had already made separate plans. Once in town I stopped and picked up a few pints of rum and arrived at Chris's place with a smile on my face. When I left, I had a bigger smile on my face and memories to put into my log. Emma and Big Don arrived later in the evening and the girls drove us back to the ship. As we had not consumed much of the rum, I decided to save it for a later date. I put the near-empty pint in my jumper pocket where it surely would be found and then removed by the duty officer, the other went into the back of my trousers and hopefully not noticed. It worked and I had a pint for later when the weather would be cold.

October 31st was a somber day, our last day in port for weeks. The girls picked up Big Don and I at the ship and we headed into Christchurch. Unfortunately, Chris had to return to her job and would be delayed until 8:00 that night. Later, the three of us picked up Chris and went for a nice dinner. With everyone tired from the last three days of excitement, we said our goodbyes. We made arrangements for our return in late December and we would have many more good times then. Big Don and I headed to another club we had heard about, but after a few beers we called it a night and back to the "old grind" we went. Tomorrow would start a new adventure.

November 1st. Left Port Lyttleton at 0930 and headed south towards Scott Island. It was cloudy with some rain and the seas a little rough. With five days and nights of hard partying, most of the crew needed to get their sea legs back under them. Today marked the beginning of the beards again so the guys would look scrubby for some time. When we return to Lyttleton in December, the girls are going to be shocked. Dumbass Shakey changed our watch schedule as there were too many RM's not doing anything and you can't have that…keep their asses busy or they will get into trouble. So, even after years of experience with this very subject, he put us on 4-hour watches. This would last a very short time after information was getting lost between watches.

As we continued on our SSE direction toward Scott Island, the weather began to show its ugly face. The temps were slowly getting cooler, it snowed most everyday and there was a new smell in the air. This new smell was pure freshness and it wasn't just the air, the water seemed much clearer, and later we would discover just how clear it really was. It's been 5 weeks since we left Seattle and we only have a day or two before we see our first ice. We are prepared as foul-weather gear including large heavy coats, hats, gloves, boots and goggles have been issued to all hands.

November 5th. Today we crossed the 60-degree parallel, so in maritime terms we are now officially a "Red Nose." We are getting close to our objective and those of us who have not been here before are acting like kids at Christmas. Shakey changed the watch schedule again. Now we are 12 on/12 off and that flat out is NOT going to work; he must have his head stuck right up his skinny ass! That schedule means the most sleep we could possible get would be 7 hours and that would require not bathing, not eating, no social life, and just who is going to take care of our assigned areas for cleaning?

November 6th. Today we got a call that the USNS Chattahoochee is stuck in ice, so we and the Glacier are on the way to get her free. OPERATION DEEPFREEZE 63…HERE WE COME!

Note: There are three US Navy icebreakers (Glacier, Edisto and the Staten Island) and one US Coast Guard icebreaker (Eastwind), along with a convoy of commercial supply ships that make up this task force. Our mission is to get these supply ships to McMurdo as quickly as possible and safely.

The Top 40 hits of the time: Ramblin' Rose, Duke of Earl, Hey Baby.

CHAPTER 8

MCMURDO, ANTARCTICA

As part of Task Force CTG 43.1, the USS Staten Island was just one of the icebreakers deployed. The USS Glacier, USS Edisto and the Coast Guard Cutter Eastwind were also in support. Their missions were in parts. The first part for all was to open a channel into McMurdo, escort the supply ships into McMurdo, and keep the channel open for further resupply during summer months. Each icebreaker had its mission after the channel was opened and the supplies were delivered to the base at McMurdo; ours was returning to Port Lyttleton, resupply and prepare for a scientific expedition in and around Palmer Peninsula. I think we got the best of the best, as running up and down that channel for three more months would be more than most could take.

Approaching Antarctica, the air and water temperatures continue to drop and we begin to see the development of "pancake ice." These creations are the beginning of saltwater forming thick layers of solid ice. Once connected, it grows and grows and grows until it is a solid mass. It wasn't long and we were in the ice. As far as the eye can see lies a mass of white ice that will for us end up reaching depths of over well over 10 feet.

All of the ships in this task force have come from ports all over the United States and each had their stops along the way. Most came from the east coast and arrived in New Zealand after passing through the Panama Canal. Now, six weeks later, we were rendezvousing in this frozen tundra and about to forge ahead into McMurdo.

The plan is fairly simple as each breaker enters the ice at different angles and will meet at a fixed point some miles closer to McMurdo. This opens cracks and allows this ice to flow out into open water and relieve some of the pressure. At this point, the main channel will begin with the Glacier, the largest icebreaker, leading the way. The theory here is to break a large piece of ice away from the mass and, once free, it will flow or be pushed out into open water. Early on this theory worked perfect.

Keep in mind we're working with the military brain here and that logic sometimes leaves one standing with a stare on their face. You see, a breaker accomplishes its task by ramming the ice, and with the brute power and weight of the ship, the ice crumbles and we move forward. So far so good; however, as you move forward the ice becomes thicker and thicker and is harder and harder to break, so a new plan is implemented. This is a bit more complicated but makes sense. The breaker now rams the ice once to the left, backs off, then rams to the right, backs off, and hits it in the middle, and the larger hunks of ice are broken off. We will be doing this for about 30 days, 24 hours a day. Back up, ram…back up, ram…back up, ram…! Below the main deck are the living quarters where one is allowed to sleep occasionally and that damn ice grinds its way aft along those very walls, sounding like Godzilla scraping his fingernails on a blackboard. And if that isn't enough, the back and forth motion will drive you nuts. As the ice gets thicker, the breaker now forces itself upon the ice (angled bow allows this to happen) so that weight and power break pieces off. So now we back up, ram, ride up, ride down...back up, ram, ride up, ride down… and they wonder why we drink!

These icebreakers are tough and were designed well; however, there was always one danger present, large chunks of ice (I'm talking tons) can come in contact with the screws (or props in laymen terms). These screws are very large and made of materials designed to not only provide raw power but would withstand such force. And by power, I mean from a standing idle to a speed of over 12 knots, those six in-line diesel-powered engines would thrust us upon that ice in about 100 yards. Amazing what happens when you throw 6500 tons onto ice.

The Glacier was the newest breaker in the fleet, had more power, weighed more, and had some design features the Navy was trying. The "screws" had been manufactured by another company, with newer technology than the rest of us. So much for that program, they have been the latest, greatest prop in the world but the rest of us just got "screwed" (I just love puns). They could not withstand the punishment. So it wasn't long and the Glacier was on its way back to Wellington, New Zealand to replace a screw. Not many ship yards in the world have a spare screw for an icebreaker just laying around, if you get my drift, so one had to be shipped all the way from the northeastern part of the USA and we're talking about five weeks for delivery. Nice to know you, you bastards! Shore duty in Wellington for at least five weeks while we freeze our asses off.

Now some major changes had to happen and Commander Price Lewis, Jr. who was in charge of Task Force CTG 43.1 was coming aboard the Staten Island and we would become the "flag" ship. Great! More work for us and by that I mean the radiomen as we know would be handling not only our traffic but his and also his Task Force. As it turned out, that extra workload gave me the opportunity to hone my skills and become a wiz on the speed key.

We now became the lead breaker and would bear the bulk of breaking into McMurdo while the other breakers would tow the supply ships up the channel and keep it clear.

When we first entered the ice, we could make about 50 miles a day. At a point short of McMurdo, we were lucky to go 100 yards a day until the ice won and we were almost two miles short of the base.

November 8, 1962. Not only has the weather gotten colder but we are all having trouble keeping track of time as there are about 22 hours of daylight, and adjusting to that is a challenge. I'm on the mid-watch and it is still light out.

November 9th. Those in charge on the bridge seem to be having trouble mastering the art of ice-breaking as we all seem to be getting stuck and often. Once the ice is broken, you must back off quickly and that moves the ice. If you linger too long, it closes in on you, and all of a sudden the suction grabs you and you become one big glob of ice. There will be many moments in this predicament before we get out of here; some would be so funny you'd laugh till you cried. We are having our first big blizzard today and the temperatures are getting colder. There will be no sunset today as before it reaches the horizon it will rise for the beginning of the new day, a very spectacular but strange site. This also marked 11 weeks since we left Seattle.

November 13th. We are off Ross Island and can see Mt. Erebus, an active volcano, the only active one in this part of Antarctica, and we can see it smoking in the distance. We are close enough to land that many penguins are now making their way to check us out. The Adelie and Emperor penguins are in this area and we will see thousands of them before we are finished. Today was a big day for many as promotions became official and as of right now I'm the only Seaman in the radio shack as Big Don and RB made Petty Officer Third Class. I will get my chance in six months but in the meantime, I will surely catch all the shit details being the junior guy.

Today we towed the Chattahoochee and Mirfak up the channel, and we are now getting closer but have a long way to go. We are getting mail about every two or three days. It's flown into McMurdo and then one of our choppers picks it up.

Today seemed to be a milestone for me as all I could think of was my buddies back home, most going to college. A little self pity of course but oh how I wished I would have buckled down and stuck with my plan to be an architect. Now I must wait for my chance. Hard to believe that Mike and I made our decision two years ago.

The days seem to be dragging and we need some action. This same old daily routine with the same old scenery can drive a grown man to tears.

November 22nd. Thanksgiving, so we'll have a good meal and some free time, which means playing cribbage, pinochle, hearts or poker while drinking coffee, tea or milk. Of course we'll have our movie at 2000 hours (8:00 p.m.) and lights out at 2200. We took the lead today as the Glacier finally left for repairs. It's nice to be the leader.

November 24th. We are getting behind schedule as this ice is very thick and the going is slow. At this point we are about two weeks behind and McMurdo badly needs the supplies we're towing in.

November 26th. We had to stop today as we had some repairs to make. Several of us got off the ship and onto the ice of Antarctica. Big Don and I did a much-needed "burn run" on the ice. The penguins were all around and many of us picked one up, and they just looked at you and stared back. They would not eat anything from us, even bread or fish. These little Adelies are only about 16 to 18 inches tall and were really quit intriguing little critters. Later a couple of very large seals slid out of the channel and Big Don thought it would be fun to ride one, gave it a try and discovered that it was, in fact, NOT a good idea. The laundry could not get the stench out of his clothes and they had to be thrown away.

By the first of December we were still about six miles away from our destination, and advancing by just yards, there was lots of work yet to be done. A few of the guys who have been through this before say it's the thickest ice they have ever seen and doubt we will make it to McMurdo. In that case, the supplies will have to be towed.

The days seem to drag by as there really is nothing new, just that constant pounding the ice or running up and down the channel. The only saving grace was that we at least got mail a couple times a week but the taste of a good brew or the sweet smell of a lovely young lady was unfortunately missing and that pleasure would be weeks away. I am surprised that the temperament of the guys seems to be quite good, not much bickering even when one loses at a game of chance. Ah, but those days will come.

Prior to us leaving Seattle, the Captain had written a letter that was sent to all wives, mothers, fathers etc., outlining what was ahead for us and recommended sending any birthday or Christmas gifts clearly marked for which event and to send them early before we left New Zealand. In that letter he asked for some to send generic Christmas gifts as some would not receive gifts from family or friends and this way there would be something under the tree for those who were left out.

December started creeping by, day by day, and the scenery didn't change. On the 9th of December, the Captain finally stopped the ship and allowed those not on watch to get off and witness the art of breaking ice from a distance. What a great break this was and those of us who could go headed to the ice. Me with my 8mm camera in hand, I knew this would be good. It was amazing to watch. One could feel the power as it crashed onto the ice, then backed up quickly and hit it again and again. Of course, the penguins showed up and after a short chase, I had another one in my hands. This time I wanted a souvenir and plucked two feathers out of his ass. I had those damn things in my log book for almost forty five years before they completely fell apart. My log book held on and, although ragged, I think it will go to my children upon my voyage to yet another place.

One thing I am accomplishing is my ability at the key. My speed is amazing and I am not asked to repeat very often, which means it's clear and uniform. RB and I have been practicing on the speed key but cannot use over the live air until we pass our qualifying test, and that won't happen until we get back to Seattle. To practice receiving code at a rapid pace, we have resorted to reading coded messages that are sent to the SUB fleet. This is much like what we learned in school but at speeds of up to 30 words a minute. It helps pass the time away during mid-watches and will help immensely when we take our tests.

December 10th. Got stuck in the ice today and had to resort to blowing our way out. Now this little trick goes like this. One gets on the ice and drills holes into the ice, then packs those holes with explosives and then BOOM! After that it takes about 60 to 70 seconds before all of the little pieces finally stop falling from the sky. The theory is that those explosions will create a crack and relieve the pressure. Sometimes it does, sometimes it doesn't, so we do the BOOM thing again.

December 11th. After having gotten free yesterday, we headed back down the channel and began towing the Mirfak up towards McMurdo to what will be the last mooring for her before offloading her supplies. Then we'll return and bring up the Chattahoochee. Today marks the third month of this journey and it's been 45 days since we were last in port. We need to get the hell out of here and soon.

The next two days were much the same; we went nowhere. We keep trying to get closer but it just isn't going to happen. I can't believe they have not given up and gotten on with the off-loading. It surely won't be much longer.

December 18th. Winter is coming and quick! The winds reached nearly 50 knots and visibility was almost nonexistent. The cold just goes right through you and you better shut the hatches quick or the whole room will freeze in just a few seconds. Keep in mind, this is the beginning of Antarctica's summer; think what it must be like in six months. Damn!

December 19th. Today the ships we towed through hell are beginning to off-load their supplies. We are about two miles from the base at McMurdo and those poor guys have to lug this gigantic load of who-knows-what to their warehouses. We did our jobs and will soon be heading back to New Zealand for much needed R & R. The Edisto pulled alongside us today and we went aboard to check out her radio room. It was smaller than ours and not as functional. Met the other radiomen, many we have been talking with via CW and voice communications. Nice to put a face to a DIT & DAH. One of those radiomen would come back into my life, actually assigned to work for me, but I found it necessary to fire him.

I spent several years in sales, and during my selling career was a District Manager for Compugraphic, the largest manufacturer of photo-typesetting equipment. Around 1979-80, there were geographical changes in some districts so I lost a few guys and gained a few. One of those was from Davenport, Iowa. As was my norm, a breakfast meeting was set for 7:30 a.m. and, as usual, I was early. I took a table, ordered coffee, grapefruit juice and English muffin (I bet I have ordered that at least a thousand times) and awaited his arrival. By 7:45 a.m., I was chomping at the bit and at 8:00 a.m. I called my boss and informed him of the situation. Good ole' George said; "fire the son-of-a-bitch!" This dude I was meeting had worked for our major competitor for several years and was tired of getting his ass kicked by our guys, so he jumped ship and was giving it a go with us. With the business behavior I was seeing, it was no wonder we were drowning him. There were no cell-phones in those days but you could find one of Ma Bell's jewels just about anywhere so that was not an excuse. A simple phone call might have saved his ass...for awhile.

When he finally showed up around 8:15 a.m., I inquired about his tardiness at which time he began to give me his side of the story. Ok, let's get on with our meeting. I got my coffee filled and proceeded to ask him a series of questions; his family, his education, his work experience, his goals, his accomplishments in business and, had he served in the Armed Forces. I always saved that for last as it is a good place to make decisions on how I feel about certain people. His answer was yes, the Navy. The Navy? What was your rate and rank? Radioman Third Class. Really? That's interesting, you mean dit's and dah's? Of course he said yes (he has no flippin idea as yet). How long were you in the service? From 61 thru early 65. Tell me about what you did, I said. Well you know, boot camp, then Radioman school, then on a ship was his reply. What kind of ship did you serve on? An icebreaker...and with that I almost went backward in my chair. This guy is a radioman who has served on an icebreaker? What was the name of the icebreaker? The USS Edisto. After I asked him where he went on that breaker, I think I went into a tizzy. He had been in Operation Deepfreeze 63 in Antarctica. I had met this dumb-ass at McMurdo!

Well I had had all I wanted of him at this point and informed him of MY WAY things would be done in MY district and he needed to pay attention. The first thing I did was assign him to work with one of my guys for a week and we would talk after he got the low-down from one of my best salesmen.

After talking with my rep and getting his feelings and then putting the heat on him, it was obvious this guy was just looking for a free ride and there was no train in our district for him to hop onto. Fellow sailor and radioman didn't mean shit! It took less than six weeks and he chose to find another vocation.

December 20th. We now know what is in our future. Tomorrow we leave for Port Lyttleton and will have several days of fantasy, fun and frolicking. We are going to be resupplied with much-needed goods and materials, refueled to the max, and take on a research group who want to gather information for the purpose of creating a US Research Station on Palmer Peninsula. Sounds like fun but first let's get to Port Lyttleton. The only bad news was that when the time came for us to head back to Seattle, we would return up the coast of South America and would miss the stops in Australia and a few of the exotic South Pacific gems.

It appeared the Staten Island was selected to go on the mission to Palmer Peninsula because of our ability to perform our duties well. We would be isolated from everyone else and really isolated from the rest of the world for over three months. That meant no mail, no resupply, no booze, no broads, and we must have good luck or we could be spending the winter there.

I must make note here about the possibility of wintering over in the ice. It takes a certain type of person who can withstand that. Before being assigned to one of these vessels, one's personal life is checked. My aunt about had a stroke when the FBI showed up at her door in the late spring of 1962 asking many questions about my background, education, etc, etc, etc. Not only did they interview her, but many of our neighbors also had been asked questions. It's clear to me that they must have missed something because I was stationed with some really strange individuals and I certainly wasn't looking forward to spending the entire winter with these morons.

December 23rd. After the mid watch, I ate a big breakfast and hit the rack for some much-needed sleep. After about four hours sleep, I awoke to a little rock-n-rollin'...it seems we have reached open water. I checked in navigation and we are at 74-18.0S & 172-23.8E heading to Port Lyttleton. We all had hoped we would be there by Christmas but that won't be happening. It's hard to believe that about five weeks ago this exact spot was at least four to five feet thick of ice.

December 24th. Christmas Eve and the lonely feelings really hit the heart. Last year at this time I was in San Diego awaiting a court-martial and now I am at the bottom of the world. Everyone seems to be in the mood except me. I really miss my family and friends, and having gotten my Dear John letter earlier this year, I don't even have a girl to think and dream of. Tonight is the big Christmas party and all the gifts will be handed out by Santa. At 2000 hours, Santa began calling out names, everyone cheered and clapped and jeered and teased and really was fun for all. But alas, there were a few of us that received token gifts. I was pleased as I was rewarded a really nice box of stationary. I wrote a thank-you letter with the first sheet of paper. After the party many of us gathered in the mess hall with our little saved hidden treasures and par-took in an adult beverage. That little bottle of rum had lasted for just this occasion.

A brief history lesson here. As I noted, early in my life things just didn't go the normal way. Divorced families were very uncommon in the 40s; raised by relatives in their 50s was like being raised by great grandparents. In the sixth grade I had two events that will clearly outline my future in such topics. Ms. O'Hara was my teacher, the best teacher I ever had, and she pushed us hard and we all responded. On a tour of a local television station and the featured class on a weekly program, we were rewarded with ice-cream sandwiches that were brought to our school and we took turns getting up and being handed ours by the show's host. My real last name started with an L but my guardians started with a W. Everything we did in Ms. O'Hara's class was in alphabetical order thus I would be, you got it, the last to get up and receive my goodies. Yep, one short! I didn't even get to lick a wrapper. That, my friends, was the way things just happened for me. In a class play later that year, we had performed the masterpiece before the student body and would again get our chance to "star" in front of parents later in the week. The "big show" was about to get started and our costumes were being brought into the classroom for us to get dressed. Yep, mine seemed to have gotten misplaced. Who in the hell would steal a Bear costume, so it was a "no show" for me. This pattern just seemed to stick with me for most of my life.

Another example of this "stroke of luck" happened after getting out of the Navy. I attempted to become a ticket agent for TWA. There were ads on the radio and in the newspaper and all those who wanted to apply were to be at the airport at 8:00 a.m. on a Saturday. There must have been 500 applicants for 10 openings. It took nearly all day for them to test each on paper and in person, and they ended up selecting 20 finalists. I made the cut and I was sure I would make it. Yep, I came in eleventh. God's truth!

Christmas Day 1962. At sea and it's a normal holiday routine. All awaiting the big dinner tonight but some will not make it as the seas are beginning to get rough and food will be the last thing on some of those minds. Good for me as I never was bothered with seasickness and that would leave more turkey for those of us who had strong stomachs.

December 26th. Seas are still very rough. We took a 39-degree roll and this will be a good lesson for the other rough waters we will end up in. Tempers are starting to show and the "lifers" are putting everyone in a foul mood. Johnston seems to be really giving us radiomen all the shit duties and is not happy with anything. Big Don and he have had several verbal confrontations, and Don's nose is getting very, very red.

Over the next few days, the seas calmed down and all hands were getting the ship ready for arrival in Port Lyttleton. Everything from top to bottom has been cleaned, re-cleaned and painted as needed. All uniforms have been cleaned and pressed, pay day and of course our pre-arrival lecture, and after having been away from the civilian world for over two months, we probably need a refresher.

December 29th. Got assigned to mess cooking today. I will be working as a cook's aide, dish washer, food prepper, or clean-up sailor for the next three months. I got the nod as each division provides at least one seaman grade member every three months for this glorious duty. The other seaman grade members of our division were radarmen, and Johnston, being a radarman, was not going to let a lowly radioman get by without sending me. I was the senior seaman in our divison but even Shakey could not change his mind.

December 30th. Pulled into Port Lyttleton and were greeted by a pier full of lovelies and bags full of mail. I kept looking for Chris but she didn't make it. I chose to work in the kitchen doing the prep work (peeling potatoes etc, etc) as we are finished for the day when that job is done, and we were usually off duty by 1400 hours. Had to finish my duties in the mess hall, shower, and then hit the beach. I tried again to reach Chris but there was no answer. When I returned to the ship, I finished going through my mail and found a letter from her. She was in Wellington for the holidays with her parents and would be back on January 3rd. That won't leave us much time together and I was so looking forward to spending some time with her.

Sure sucks having mess cooking as I have to stay aboard and finish with all the prep work for all of the day's meals. At least there is not a much to do as over half the guys go on liberty at 1300 hours. That saves Alex and I fifty pounds of potatoes plus any onions, carrots or other fresh vegetables that need to be peeled.

New Year's Eve 1962. Stayed on board until 1800 hours, as it was my turn to remain until evening chow had been served. Big Don and the guys hit the beach at 1300 and were on a mission to find a killer New Year's party for us all to attend. Chuckles stayed until we could go together, and after a shower we were in a cab headed for Fun City. Big Don had called Chuckles and told him to meet them at the EM Club and we all would then head to a party that was being thrown in our honor. Nice of them blokes, I'd say! Beer, Booze and Broads...going to have some fun tonight!

After a few brews at the EM Club and briefing on how, when and where this party was at, we hailed a couple of cabs and were on our way. We arrived in this nice neighborhood somewhere in Christchurch and were greeted by a couple who were in their 30's (guessing at the age, but older than us) and invited in. There were a few other couples at this time but one major thing was missing! The Beer and Booze was on the patio but the Broads were missing, except those already attached. We all were enjoying our drinks and exchanging conversation about a variety of topics but it was going on 2100 hours (9:00 p.m.) and still no Broads, and if we're going to have fun, things had better start happening soon or we'll have to head back to Party City and re-engage…if you get my drift!

At the strike of 2100 hours, the door bell rang and "Shangrila" came walking through the door. All of a sudden we were outnumbered and we loved the odds. They came storming into the den and, like shopping for a dress, they picked out their favorite sailor. This was my kind of shopping. An absolutely stunning belle came over and sat right on my lap, kissed my cheek and said, "Hi! I'm Beverly…HOW DO YOU DO!" After getting the girls their favorite adult beverages, the music began, dancing started, and getting to know one another became a form of art. What had started out as a DUD of a party turned into a "FIVE STAR EVENT."

Many smiles were created tonight. HAPPY NEW YEAR!

CHAPTER 9

JANUARY 1, 1963

What a great way to start the new year. Here I am in New Zealand with not one but two lovelies and very little time to enjoy their company. This is not a problem, and most would be overjoyed, but how do I juggle this dilemma? Chris will be back soon and I really want to see her again but Beverly is here, now, and ready for action. My uncle always said, "a bird in the hand is worth two in the bush" so I'm going with that...I'm calling Beverly.

Most everyone was feeling the pains of last night but we mustered up the strength and headed to town for a couple of "fix-me-uppers." With our visit coming closer to the end, we decided to take it slow tonight and we were back at the ship before midnight.

January 2nd. Tonight will be redemption night, pay-backs are hell! Aboard ship it is a beehive of action with loading of supplies, scientists moving in with their equipment, finishing needed repairs, and good old fashion anticipation of what is coming in the next three months. When we leave Port Lyttleton, New Zealand, we will be isolated in Antarctica until we enter Valpariso, Chili in mid March so we must have everything we need on board before we depart. There are no "do-overs" on this mission.

At this point, most everyone has found themselves a favorite haunt or that special gal to enjoy the rest of their time here in our little paradise. Lots of guys are being picked up at the ship and their smiling faces won't be seen until tomorrow. Since Chris is not back yet, Big Don suggested we head to the Kooper Kay in downtown Christchurch as they have a great band, lots of action, and some really good food, so off we go.

The place was crawling with broads so we danced with several but shied away from making serious contact. A guy can only handle just so much, and Chris was due tomorrow. After about two hours of fun, in walks this group of "lifers" from the ship led by none other than Johnston. I could see the hair rise on the back of Big Don's neck and that beacon nose beginning to glow crimson red…he was pissed and looking for pay-back. It took him about five minutes before he approached Johnston and shared words, and that's when he popped Big Don. Oh SHIT! Here we go. In a flash they're trading punches, the guys in the band are going crazy, and the next thing I know both are on the ground right in the middle of the bandstand. Johnston had gotten the best of Big Don and thrown him to the ground, then pounced on him and began punching again. OK, fun is over! I grab the back of Johnston's jumper, pulled back like I was trying to stop a horse and explored his head with my right fist. Johnston's buddies were about to enter the fray but the Bobbies showed up and the fight was over. They made us pay our tabs and escorted us out. They were nice and kept us separated but told us our night was over in Christchurch, and to catch cabs and head back to the ship. Big Don and I were first, and back to the Staten Island we went.

The next day it was obvious who had won the battle as Johnston looked like he had fallen down the stairs and Big Don just had a bruised ear. Like I said, pay-backs can be hell. The feud seemed to end that night and things were a bit mild for the next few months.

January 3rd. Got that call I had been waiting for as I was summoned to the quarter-deck for a message and BINGO! Chris is back in town and requested a call back. DONE, met her for dinner in Christchurch at 1800 hours. Over dinner we talked about family and the holidays, the ship's trip to Antarctica and what we're doing tonight. We soon headed for her car, stopped for a bottle of rum and headed to her house for the evening. Looks like yet another smile is coming to my face tonight. We enjoyed what would be our last time together that evening and I had to head back around midnight. I called a cab and we said our good-byes, and the little bloke and I chatted all the way back to the ship. I had a broad smile on my face but I was beginning to feel a scratch in my throat and a bit warm. Was it love or something else?

During the night I got much worse as my throat got raw, the sweat started pouring off my face and I was burning up. I could hardly sleep and that never happens as I could sleep through a thunderstorm and never move.

January 4th. I could hardly move in the morning and felt like I could die at any moment. My throat was raw and it felt like someone had just poured gasoline down my gullet. I quickly got to Doc (the corpsman) and we headed to sick-bay. One look at my throat and he knew I was in trouble, and after taking my temperature he summoned the doctor. I had tonsillitis and my 103 temp was going to ruin my last day in New Zealand. After a shot in the ass, I was sent back to my bunk and put on "restriction," taken off my mess-cooking duties and had to say good bye to "Shangri-La" from the ship. Not a very heartwarming way to leave. I called Chris and she wanted to drive down but with my restriction, that just couldn't happen. We said our final good-byes.

After we departed for Palmer Peninsula, we would not get mail for about ten weeks. I then had a letter from her detailing our time together and with her hopes that we would meet again. I didn't have the heart to respond, but over the years as I looked at my log, I couldn't help but have that smile on my face just thinking about her.

January 5th. We departed Port Lyttleton at 1015 hours with a pier full of young ladies, hearts broken no doubt, all waving and yelling "goodbye." We are now heading to a place that's over 4,000 miles away and we will see nothing but rough water, icebergs, whales, birds, and each other. Talk about isolated duty, we are in for it and don't even realize it.

January 7th. After a few normal days at sea, we crossed the time zone again and now will have two Mondays on our calendar. In the radio shack we finally were able to pick up KOMA out of Oklahoma City. KOMA was a 50,000 watt AM station and they played all the latest TOP-40 hits. We were only able to pick it up at night and we patched it throughout the ship for all to enjoy. Some of those songs really sounded strange as we had not heard many of them. Our position today is 47.50S & 179.14W.

Got another shot today and have five more to go, but the doctor says I'm safe and took me off restriction, so I'll be back with mess-cooking duties tomorrow.

January 16th. Since leaving New Zealand, we have traveled through the Ross Sea, the Amundsen Sea and the Bellingshausen Sea. The weather is much colder and the sky has one color, gray. The seas have been a bit rough and it never seems to stop snowing. This sure has been a boring ride so far. We are beginning to see more icebergs now. The radarmen are also beginning to plot them as they move, as we don't want a repeat of the Titanic. By the time we leave this abyss, we will have seen thousands of them - some small and many ten to twenty times our size. We have traveled over 14,500 miles since we left Seattle and have thousands of miles to go before we return. Tomorrow we'll be at our first of many stops on or near Palmer Peninsula.

January 17th. We arrived at Adelaide Island and the ship is again acting like a bee-hive in preparation for the research guys to go ashore and do their thing, whatever the hell that might be. The water looks muddy brown and seems to swirl in about seven different directions, but this will change. The scenery is magnificent and it looks like an Ansel Adams image. We will see these patterns continue throughout our journey here, mostly black and white, ice and rock. This topography will be a problem later.

January 18th. The research group spent the day exploring different regions of Adelaide Island. We know very little of what they are doing. They go ashore on our LCVP (landing boat), then return, we move to another location and again they go ashore, repeat, repeat, repeat. Boring!

January 19th. We arrived at the Bristol base, which was much like McMurdo, and launched the Greenland cruiser and the LCVP filled with supplies. The Captain and crew exchanged pleasantries and they returned.

We've been gone for 17 weeks now and have almost 11 more weeks to go before we return to Seattle.

January 20th. We are still in the vicinity of Adelaide Island in Marguerite Bay. We are the first ship in this bay since 1941. The water is very deep and the mountains soar towards the sky. With the sky so low and gray, it's a very weary scene. We will be in places the next few months that will equal this view and others that will blow our minds away.

January 21st. En route to Anvers Island.

January 22nd. We arrived at Anvers Island at 0800, a very beautiful scene and one of the very small islands that has thousands of penguins frolicking on and off the ice flows. They are like little children playing at the pool and are quite amused at our presence. Later in the day, winds went from 10 knots to over 60 knots in less than ten minutes and we had to pull back out to sea. Fortunately, the research team was on board or we would have had to leave them on shore until we could return. This scenario will happen again and one incident came close to being tragic.

January 23rd. We returned to Arthur Bay, Anvers Island at 0800 and, with the sun out and bright, the research group headed to shore and spent the day doing whatever the hell it is they do.

Alex and I have been busy learning the art of peeling potatoes, carrots and turnips. As we leave the galley for the day, we check the menu for tomorrow's meal and that tells us what our day is going to be like in the morning. Most, and I mean most, meals come with potatoes and with our crew that means 150 pounds need to be peeled. When we left Port Lyttleton, the reefer (LARGE refrigerator) was filled with potatoes, carrots, turnips, fresh greens, and eggs. When I say filled, I mean to the fricken top! We have this monstrosity that some idiot created as a potato peeler, cylindrical in design, with the interior finished like course sandpaper. The theory is, put about 25 pounds of spuds in the damn thing, turn it loose, and it will jostle them to remove the skin. Well it kinda' does, but it leaves the eyes and when you finish, you still have to remove the eyes, and worse yet, clean that damn monster and that takes longer than peeling the son-of-a-bitches. Besides, if we were just peeling the potatoes, no one would dream of something else for us to do. There will be more on potatoes later.

January 25th. Still at Anvers Island but pulled out of Arthur Bay and headed to the other side of the island. The mountains here rise several thousand feet and are absolutely stunning...so far the most beautiful place we've been.

During the next few days, we stopped at several no-name islands just to explore but we are working our way in a northeasterly direction on the west side of Palmer Peninsula.

January 28th. We reached the Argentine Islands and will be in this area for a few days. Not as scenic as our last stop.

January 31st. On the move today and came across a British resupply ship early in the day, and then around 1300 she came by again. Both crews were taking pictures of each other. They passed us about twenty feet away so we all got a close up look at each other.

The weather pattern is changing with temps during daytime hours around 30-35 degrees and the nights are getting darker, all of which means winter is going to show its ugly head very soon.

February 1st. Around noon we came upon Paradise Harbor and we ended up spending a few days exploring.

Febuary 3rd. Today is my second anniversary in the Navy. There will be no bands playing or cake and ice-cream served but at least I am halfway through my tour of duty.

It got to a point where most of us had no clue as to where we were. We would anchor and the research guys would go ashore, come back, and we would weigh anchor and move, and this could go on for a few days. Stop and move, stop and move. And with everything being black and white, it was hard to keep track of just where in the hell you were.

Each day after leaving the galley I would get my shower and go to the radio shack. I missed being part of that but always got to send messages and keep my skills moving in the right direction. Besides, most of the guys hated sitting at the key and pounding the dit's and dah's. RB and I were the ones who sent the majority of our traffic for the whole cruise. We both seemed to always be on someone's shit list, but we were damn good at what we were trained to do.

Our off-duty activities were always the same. There was a movie every night on the mess deck and always a card game going, usually cribbage and/or pinochle. The only other thing one could do was read, and if you had not prepared your private library prior to leaving port, you were in big trouble. I loved game playing but I began to really enjoy reading more meaningful books. Real people, places and things, and to this day I still love reading books about those very subjects. I cannot see any reason to read fiction. Hell, that's what we all live every day so why read about it?

One thing that created a huge amount of excitement was the HAM radio room. Frenchie was a licensed HAM operator and had made several contacts all over the world. Every night he would make contact with another HAM in California and make phone patches. These patches gave crewmen the opportunity to talk to loved ones back home. Now this is what you call POWER. If you want to talk to Betty Lou, you had better not piss off the radiomen…if you get my drift. Now this was not like picking up a phone and dialing the number; it was much more complicated than that. It was one-way talking and the guy in California had to be on his toes. When you made a statement you had to say "over." Then, and only then, could the other person talk. It took some getting used to but was fun for those who got the privilege.

February 7th. Today the research guys went fishing, baiting hooks and lowering the lines into depths unknown. They caught fish that had no eyes, no scales, and were not only weird looking but were of colors hard to describe.

February 8th. Today we were at Brabant Island and Wiencke Island and surveyed Dorian Bay. Same old stuff and we all want to go home.

Around 0200, I was awakened for my turn in the HAM shack. I was thrilled as most were. After entering the HAM shack, I was handed the "mike" and began. My aunt was totally confused as she had just been awakened from a collect call from California so the first thing she asked was "are you home?" She just never did get it. The really weird thing was we were in the same time zone, 2:00 a.m., she in Kansas City and I in Antarctica.

February 11th. We are still island hopping and counting the days till we get the hell out of here. We are headed to Deception Island, an active volcano that, through its volcanic activity, created a natural harbor. This Island has been used for years as a whaling station.

February 12th. Arrived at Deception Island around 0800 and entered her natural bay. Once in the towering walls of this wonder of nature, you could see the steam rising and feel the heat, although very slight. There were remains of what used to be a massive whaling operation and a wrecked whaling ship almost completely decayed. One of the South Shetland Islands, it rises 1900 feet and it last erupted in 1970.

February 13th. Headed to Yankee Bay. I was now spending my free time studying for the Radioman Third Class Petty Officers test tomorrow, so went to bed early for some much-needed rest.

February 15th. Test was canceled yesterday for some reason but was held today in the mess hall. The Radioman test was at least eighty percent electronics and twenty percent communications, and knowing that electronics was not my strength in school, I doubt that I will make the grade. Getting promotions is getting harder and harder, and just because you pass the test doesn't guarantee you'll make it. We are underway and heading to the east side of Palmer Peninsula and into the Weddell Sea.

February 16th. Came to a halt today as we approached an ice shelf, and we need to find a way around it rather than through it. The choppers went up and are searching for an opening.

February 17th. On the move again and headed to Snow Island. The word is out that we are going to get off this tub and the plan is to have a party, a good old fashioned BBQ and BEER. Our big surprise as the Captain had the adult beverages brought aboard as he knew we would need a break at some point, and now after six weeks of this crap, it's the perfect time.

February 18th. Anchored off Snow Island and the weather is terrible. With the snow, wind and cold, it looks like no party today.

February 20th. Finally the weather cleared and was perfect for the party. The cooks and a few "lifers" went ashore and set up the gear and started cooking, and when they're ready we'll get boated ashore. After what seemed like hours, we finally got our feet on land. The smell of the BBQ permeated the air and after standing in line for my beer ration, I felt like I was in heaven. Most everyone just explored the area and found little souvenirs. I found several loose seal teeth and jaw bones with teeth. We also discovered that this island is a place where whales come to die as we found the skeletal remains of a few. I posed with two large rib bones but was not allowed to bring them home. The party was a great relief and settled the crew down just a bit, but it ended way too soon.

Note about adult beverages aboard US Navy ships. NOT ALLOWED. I don't know what the rules are today but in my day it was a NO-NO. Our Captain was allowed to store the beer under lock and key for special occasions, off ship, due to our isolated duty.

For the next few days we went small-island hopping and the research team spent more time in the LCVD than on land. No one really knows what they are looking for but they bring boxes of what they find back to the ship and into their little private lab, and close the door. Seems it's a big secret.

Our time here is getting short and we will be leaving soon, and that's a good thing as winter is almost here and the weather is getting bad. It's getting colder and it snows all the time.

Feb 23rd. During the night while anchored off one of the small islands, an iceberg floated right up next to the ship. This baby was huge and the "panic button" went off. One of the choppers was launched, and visually could see that we were not in danger and could pull away without any problems. We were only about 20 feet away from this beauty...what a site. After the photo shoot, we slowly pulled away from the iceberg and headed back to Anvers Island. It seems the research guys want to spend more time there. Must have found a honey hole.

February 28th. Today was a day many of us had waited for the whole cruise. One of our officers was a gun enthusiast and belonged to gun club back home. He arranged for us to buy guns while in Antarctica, and not only would we get them tax free, but because of the gun club and quantity purchased, we would get discounts. When my turn came, my dream gun got ordered, a Winchester 30-30. We would receive our guns when we returned to Seattle and I couldn't wait. That American-made legend still hangs on my gun rack and will be passed on to one of my grandsons.

At this point, those damn potatoes were getting very ripe. A rotten potato smells like crap and when handled, the liquid from the rotten potatoes sticks to your hands and your clothing…so basically, you run around smelling like shit! A 50-lb bag would now only yield about 30 lbs of edible potatoes; the other 20 lbs would go in the garbage. Each day would get worse so Alex and I came to a very simple solution to this problem…get rid of them! So each morning as we retrieved our daily serving of potatoes, one bag to the kitchen and one bag "in the drink" (jargon for someone or something that falls into the water).

Being dark and nobody roaming the decks at 0400, it really presented no real worries of being caught. They would sink and the problem would diminish very quickly. No more potatoes…no more problem.

One morning our order was not only potatoes, but carrots were also on the menu. At this point in time, those carrots were like rubber. They were no longer firm, bright orange vegetables…they were greenish-looking rubber sticks. Again, problem solved and "in the drink" they went, one bag a day.

While island hopping, the ship would stop, launch the LCVP, then retrieve the LCVP and be on to the next location. One of these "special" mornings, Alex and I made the managerial decision that the carrots had to go. Only four or five 20-lb bags remained and they were worthless as an eating object so they had to go. At that very moment, the ship engines slowed, and we stopped. PROBLEM! Rotten carrots float! Yep, 20-lbs of rotten carrots FLOAT. The JIG WAS UP! We were CAUGHT! But luck was on our side as the OD on the "bridge" stopped too early and we were on our way in just a few seconds. Not to be deterred, we were at it again the next morning and soon the pile of potatoes was being reduced, but we had a ways to go yet.

A few days after the carrot incident, more potatoes had been thrown overboard and we were heading towards the galley with shoulders full of rotten bags of spuds when a voice from the bridge said, "LEE!" Instantly OH SHIT was the only thing on my mind.

It seems that Lt. Thomas who was the OD at the time, had stepped outside to catch a breath of fresh air and watched our little performance in action. He strolled down the ladder (steps) and inquired as to why we were throwing good Navy potatoes into the drink. I knew our asses were in deep do-do so I had to give my best delivery possible. Again my luck was with me. This officer had been an enlisted man and, after his term ended, had gone back to college. He then returned to the Navy as an officer, and was my Division Officer. He knew what it was like to be on our side of the ship.

I straightforwardly explained the reality of what was going on and the whys and what-fors of our plan. He paused, like he was in deep thought. Our hearts were in our throats for what seemed like hours, then he calmly looked at both of us and simply said, "Gentlemen, I like potatoes. See to it I have them as long as possible." He turned and went back to the bridge.

There was never another word about it, but you can bet your ass he had his potatoes for as long as it was possible. Now that is what I call a "good" officer. He could have made our lives miserable for a very long time.

March 1st. Arrived back at Arthur Harbor, Anvers Island around 0800 hours and the research team went ashore for about an hour. Upon their return, we weighed anchor and headed back to Paradise Harbor. The seas are beginning to show their power and in open water swells are 4-6 feet. This round-bottom ship doesn't like that. It's called rock-n-roll!

March 2nd. Weather is really bad, and winter is coming fast and furious. Once at Paradise Harbor, we came across the Chilean ship Pilito Pardo. Our Captain was invited aboard the Pilito Pardo, and he boarded the Greenland Cruiser and the two captains exchanged whatever it is captains exchange. The snowy conditions didn't allow any pictures as it was almost a full-scaled blizzard. We soon departed for the South Shetland Islands.

March 3rd. The weather almost bit us in the ass today. We've been lucky so far, and even with a few close calls, everything has turned out okay. Today, however, luck was not on our side. After arriving in the South Shetland Islands, the research team headed ashore after which the blizzard got intense. It was almost a complete white-out and showing no signs of letting up. The team was lost! Time was running out and we needed to leave soon. After several hours of total panic, the crew of the LCVP finally located them and they struggled to find their way back to the ship. Today's episode just might be a precursor as to what lies ahead.

March 4th. The weather cleared. The research team went back for yet another exploration and returned without any drama.

March 5th. We are still in the South Shetland Islands and preparing to depart for Seattle via Valpariso, Chili. After meeting with several of the officers and the research team, the decision was "job done - let's go home," and at 1600 hours we were on our way.

I can tell you everyone was ready to head home. This has been a long voyage and these last two months of total isolation with no mail, no booze, no broads (we did have two beers at the BBQ), it's just about more than one man can take. We have over 6,000 miles before we dock in Seattle and at approximately 13 knots, that's one helluva long boat ride.

We are heading into what is considered the most dangerous waters in the world. Remember, we are leaving with severe winter storms all around us and these ice-breakers were not designed for cruising; they were built to break ice. The round bottoms resemble a football and when fully loaded sit quite deep in the water, which helps with the weight ratio. We have used thousands of gallons of fuel so we have come out of the water a few feet and that will just be a little added problem crossing the passage.

This experience is hard to explain as there is virtually no reference for one to compare. We were but a very, very small percentage of people who had or will have the same opportunity to view this majestic continent with towering mountain ranges, crystal-clear waters filled with giant icebergs, abundant wildlife, and with danger around every corner. Oh how I would loved to have had a digital camera as my pictures will prove to be of little value to show the grandeur of this wonderland.

The top county hits of the time: Ring of Fire, From a Jack to a King, Love's Gonna Live Here. The Top 40 hits of the time: Devil in Disguise, If I had a Hammer, Louie Louie, Hey Paula.

Author

Author Holding a Penguin

Getting Close to Antarctica

Houseboat, Me and Pod

Iceberg Pt Barrow, Alaska

McMurdo

One of our Helicopters, USS Staten Island

Polar Bear

Rough Water

Whalebones

CHAPTER 10

ARGENTINA

March 6th. Heading Home. Our first day was certainly different than the past two months as there were no flight quarters, no penguins, and we saw our last Antarctic icebergs. The seas were fairly calm but we all know what's coming; it's just a matter of time. Over the course of the next five weeks, we'll go from freezing temperatures, through the roughest waters we'll ever experience, have fantastic liberty in Valparaiso, suffer desert-like heat at the equator, visit San Diego, and then be greeted like "rock stars" when we reach Pier 91 in Seattle. Lots of emotions and release of tension will happen during this time, but when it's all over, most of us will be better men and will certainly have something to share with our friends, family, children and grandchildren.

March 7th. During the night the seas began to growl and during the day got very rough as we took several 30 and 40-degree rolls. Already many guys are rushing to the head to visit the bowls and hopefully will make it there before upchucking. By the end of the day, we had crossed Drake's Passage and are heading up the west coast of South America.

March 8th. The seas got worse today, and not only are the rolls larger than those yesterday, we are now pitching furiously through these troublesome waters. It's impossible for the galley to serve meals in these conditions.

The cooks attempted to provide sandwiches and buckets of saltines. It got so bad the coffee urns, the life blood of all sea-going sailors, had to be shut down.

March 9th. The first part of the day was about the same, rough and pitching wildly. We recorded a 48-degree roll, and in these waters, that's close to putting the yardarm in the water. Around noon the seas finally began to calm down and the ship again started to come alive. The coffee urns were started and the galley was again back in swing. The cleanup after a storm like this is monstrous and everyone "turns-to" (military jargon for "get your ass busy") with swabs and buckets, and in no time we were ship-shape again.

Waters are still rough but we were back to functional, and the nightly bingo games were played and the movie was shown as normal. The highlight tonight was the beard-judging contest, which was a comic event to be sure, with jokes about each guy who entered. Prizes were awarded for the longest, most creative and, of course, the ugliest. It was surely an event that was much needed to liven all of us up.

March 10th. After the beard-judging contest, the seas began to get rougher again, and during the night they stormed back and we again took 40+ degree rolls. We took our largest roll during the night; a nerve-racking 58-degree was recorded. I can still remember the ship shaking as it struggled to come upright. The pitching was so bad that the screws would come out of the water as we tumbled down the other side of huge swells. The noise and vibrations could be heard throughout the ship. But as the day went on, the seas began to calm and we would finally be out of danger.

During this storm, the galley was basically closed. This of course freed Alex and me from any duties in the galley so I got to spend time back in the radio shack relieving my sick brothers. Again, the cooks and a few mess cooks made sandwiches and provided boxes of saltines to help ease sick stomachs. My guess, over 90 percent of the crew fell sick. Chuckles and I were the only radiomen who did not suffer from this malady at all and we thought of the adventure as being like a gigantic roller-coaster ride.

We spent part of the 9th, all of the 10th, and into the early part of the 11th standing watch. I remember being so tired that I saw only black and white for several hours; we both were like rag dolls.

Being sick does not relieve one from their appointed duties and those who suffered less would help out their cohorts when possible. The ones who suffered the worst (in my opinion) are the guys on the bridge. They are at the highest point of activity on the ship and can see what is in front of them. The helmsman must keep the ship on course, usually into the face of the storm. I can only imagine how tired those guys were after even a four-hour watch.

March 11th. After spending two long days in the radio shack, I'm back to the galley and those damn rotten potatoes. We got the "word" that we all did not want to hear, "we are going to be a day late getting to Valpo." That storm pushed us so hard we lost ground (water) so everyone is moaning and groaning. The weather has changed for sure and we reached 63 degrees today with the sun shining bright, and by the afternoon it felt tropical to all of us.

March 12th. Everyone is busy getting this TUB cleaned up for our arrival back to civilization. Cleaning, painting, and polishing everything in sight, and with that activity going, Alex and I are happy to be peeling potatoes. The weather is unbelievable and the temperament of the whole crew is joyous.

March 13th. Another day of preparation for arrival and, as expected, we all got our "lecture." This time the Captain blessed us with his words of wisdom, instructions on the use of condoms, and behavior - topics that no one is paying attention to. All we want to know is, where are the broads, booze and beer? But of course, we will all obey those directions I'm sure. The anticipation for this arrival is worse than a five-year old child waiting for Santa. I think the night will take years to pass.

Keep in mind that the world was in turmoil with communism growing across the globe, Vietnam beginning to become a nightmare, and Cuba a never-ending threat with its alliance with USSR. The Captain warned us about the Communists trying to take over Chile and there were areas we needed to avoid at all costs as they would love take a cute little sailor boy hostage. He of course named a few areas but I really wonder if anyone paid much attention. I know I didn't and that little error in judgment would cause Big Don and I a bit of trouble down the road.

March 14th. Valparaiso, Chile. We arrived at 0830 to a pier that was a beehive of activity with fresh supplies (great, more stinking potatoes), dozens of huge mail sacks (we haven't had mail since January 5th), and of course the usual dignitaries. Alex and I were up at 0400 and had our duties done by 1100, which gave us two full hours to get ready to PARTY. Before the noon meal, which no one gave a damn about, guys were busy checking the coastline for the first place to start the action. We all knew that once our feet hit solid ground, the lovelies would not be far and we could see the closest place to grab that much-needed cerveza (beer).

At 1300 the ship exploded with liberty-bound sailors. It was a thundering herd of cooped-up, thirsty, horny rabbits for sure. At this point, no one gave a shit about their mail (they could read those letters later); beer, booze and broads were the only things on our minds. Chuckles, Big Don, Widner, RB, Freddie and I hit the bar at the end of the pier and I do believe we each had at least two down by the count of ten. Damn that tasted good and after a few more we were headed to solve our next problem.

As soon as we got out of the shipyards, there was a giant traffic circle around a very large fountain where the action went in all directions. We stood there wondering which way we should go when all of sudden, out of a cloud of dust, a Jeep appeared. With horn blaring and broads hanging all over it, they waved and motioned to us which way we needed to go. Problem solved! About two blocks down one of those many streets, we not only found where these lovelies frolicked but several other such havens to explore.

At this point in a sea-going sailor's life and after having spent months all alone in a desolate location, no instructions are needed. Need I say more? RB made his decision quickly as he knew they were in love with him, thus he would spend time with each. And damn if he didn't give it the good old college try. I didn't see much of RB during our stay in Valpo; he was way too busy getting acquainted with his harem.

By the end of the day, after visiting three or four such places of entertainment, Big Don and I broke away from the others and headed down another street. We soon were out of the bordello area and came across this little bar with the name YAKO glowing in bright neon yellow. Down two steps, we entered a quaint little cocktail lounge that certainly looked out of place being this close to the bordellos, and quickly ordered a drink.

Before long, two young ladies strolled in, all decked out to kill, and sat down at a little table not far from us. They did not appear to be Hispanic and soon we heard them speaking in German. That seemed strange to us so naturally we needed to ask (sailors do that you know). We soon found out they worked at the German embassy in Santiago, were on assignment in Valparaiso, and would be here for several months. They both spoke perfect English as well as Spanish, and they looked like the ideal match for Big Don and I.

They soon invited us to sit down and join them, and of course we obliged. Helen and Gwen, what lovely names and so easy to remember. We not only were going to have fun with these ladies but they would also show us places in the area that we were not supposed to be in. We spent hours with them in the YAKO, and soon it was nearly midnight and we had to head back to the ship. We gathered the much-needed phone numbers and agreed to get together soon. Looks like Big and I are going to like Valparaiso.

March 15th. Today was my day to stay aboard until after the evening meal. There were not many dining with us now that we were in port so I was soon showered, dressed and ready for some action. Left the ship around 1800 and headed to the YAKO hoping to find Big Don and the girls. The bartender told me to have a drink as they would soon be back. Once back at the YAKO, they were ready to have some fun. They called a cab and we headed to an unknown area of Valparaiso. The girls were taking us to a fabulous night club with live music and dancing.

When we arrived, the cabbie pulled behind the building and after much chatter between he and the girls (in Spanish), we headed in via the back door. I didn't, nor did Big Don, think much about it as we were looking for some fun. The place was hopping, music was live, and the drinks were fantastic. We danced, we sang, we laughed and had a ball. After about an hour, the cabbie came running in the back door. He had a strange look on his face, and soon he and the girls were having a heated conversation with worried looks on their faces. Big Don looked at me and I looked at Big Don with rather serious concern our faces.

The girls quickly paid the tab and said, "let's go, NOW!" We were quickly out the back door, leaving perfectly good drinks sitting on the table, and into the cab. Gwen told us to be quiet and sit low in the cab. HOLY SHIT! WHAT IS GOING ON?

As we pulled out of the alley, we soon learned why the quick departure. A gigantic march with people in white uniforms and masks, white flags with white crossed hammer and sickle, and carrying an array of weapons were coming down the street. The music created by cymbals and horns was deafening, and their cause was not in doubt. This was a Communist march and we were right in the middle of it. I think the Captain told us about this! The cabbie, who knew the girls and was hired by the embassy, saved our asses. Back to the YAKO we went. After a few drinks, the girls decided we needed to spend some private time together, so Big Don and I would see each other tomorrow, each with smiles on our faces.

This would be our last day with Helen and Gwen as they were headed back to Santiago for a meeting and they doubted they would be back before we left for home. We had gotten really lucky finding these two educated and professional gals who spent their time to show us an unforgettable experience in a strange place. They really put excitement and smiles on our faces, in more ways than one.

March 16th. With the girls gone for now, Big Don and I had to find something new to explore. Four or five of the guys from our division had heard about the casino just outside of Valpo, so a trip was being readied.

About fifteen of us grabbed cabs and headed for the action. Once in this quaint little villa, we departed the cabs and boarded horse-drawn carriages and headed to partyville.

A massive, extravagant, castle-like building awaited us. Limos and carriages pulled up to the palatial steps that led to the elegant entry. Once inside, the elegance was overwhelming; however, it didn't stop us from finding the bar.

Ace, an old salt who knew the ropes, was our leader in this adventure. A character for sure, who was loved by his shipmates, would show us the way. Ace had spent about 12 years in the Navy as a Radarman and was a Third Class Petty Officer. He should have been a Chief Petty Officer, but situations like this always caused him problems.

As he led us into the casino, we followed like little ducklings. At the entry was a guy dressed like a guard at the Vatican, and everyone had to have his blessing before entry. Once at his feet, Ace who was in the lead, was stopped and informed that we were not allowed in the casino. What??? It seems we were not properly dressed for such occasions. We were not in tuxedos as required and thus we could not enter. And that's when the shit hit the fan!

Ace gave it his best shot, explaining that in the USA, any military man dressed in uniform is considered in formal attire and that he could address the President at any formal event. The guard didn't think much of his explanation and ordered us to leave at once. Well, that didn't sit well and soon there was a ruckus. Whistles blowing and clubs in hand, we were soon outnumbered and surrounded. The police escorted us out of the casino and into awaiting cabs. We were sent on our way and told never to return. To hell with them...they were snobs anyway.

We went back to our haunts and finished the night with way too much libation in our gullets. Tomorrow morning will be bad for our bodies and much coffee will be needed for sure.

March 17th. Big Don and I decided that since the girls were still in Santiago, a shopping trip would be in order and we would become true tourists. We flagged a cab and headed to Vina Del Mar. This was an upscale residential area with boutiques, quaint restaurants and entertainment.

Alpaca was the fabric of choice, and here in Chile was very affordable. Big Don wanted to buy his girl (whom he would soon marry) an alpaca sweater, so we found ourselves in one of the many boutiques. The prices were about 50% of what they would cost in the USA and the selections were unbelievable. I bought one for my aunt, and one for an old school mate and friend, Julie. Both of these gals adored sweaters and I knew they would be hits, as birthdays would soon be coming. Besides, I needed to start schmoozing someone back home and Julie fit the bill.

After our shopping spree we searched for a place with the renowned Chilean steaks. These steaks came from cows raised in carefully selected fields, bellies rubbed to keep them calm and treated like babies their whole lives. Once slaughtered, the meat became a delicacy and sought after by connoisseurs around the world. Again, here in Chile, the prices were very reasonable.

The meal will always be remembered. Having been raised in Kansas City with its many famous steak houses, I thought I knew what a good steak was like. To this day, I believe that was the best steak I ever ate, bar none.

After dinner we wandered around and finally found a quiet little bar. We ordered drinks and soon struck up a conversation with a gentleman who spoke perfect English. After chatting for some time, he invited us to a private party. Being a little nervous about strange places, he assured us that everything was on the level, and we soon made some new friends and we were their guests. We stayed until it was time for us to head back to the ship.

Our cab got us back at 2357...three minutes to spare. Damn, that was close. Once aboard we found out the Captain extended liberty until 0200. We dropped our purchases off, and back we went to the YAKO hoping the girls may have returned. They had not, so we just enjoyed what little time we had left and pounded down more booze as we would be leaving tomorrow for the long ride home.

Valparaiso was a memory that will always be in my mind. We never heard from the girls and that's probably for the good. It would have been nice to spend a few more days as there were many places to explore, just not enough time. I would later return to this part of South America, but not back to Chile. My next visit would be later in life, by air, with Argentina and Brazil being on my itinerary.

Top country hits of this time: Ruby Ann, The End of the World, Abilene. The Top 40 hits of the time: Dominique, Sugar Shack, Surf City, It's My Party.

CHAPTER 11

ON TO SAN DIEGO

Four days! That's what we got for spending sixty-eight days at sea with no contact with the outside world. Damn those days went by fast but we all crammed as much fun as possible into those four days and we'll never forget the adventure.

March 18th. We departed Valparaiso, Chile at 0900 for the long ride to San Diego. It's going to be boring compared to what we've been through but the anticipation of getting back to Seattle is overwhelming for many. Several members of the crew are married with families and it will be over seven months away from them by the time we dock at Pier 91. Most of us are suffering from being over-served and are dragging our asses around.

March 19th. Seems the buzz around the ship is "who is going to see the Doc first." The Captain warned us about condoms, and the cause and effect for not using them, and lots of guys are sweating bullets. RB should seriously be on the top of the list as I think he spent all four days trying to service the whole bordello. It was easy getting back into the sea-going routine and things went smoothly, but we need to get this tub ready for the dreaded "inspection" when we get to San Diego, and that means scraping, painting, fixing, and whatever else the Captain wants.

March 20th. Held GQ just to get the crew on their toes. Of course, the XO (executive officer, second in command) didn't like our performance so we did it again. He's such an asshole! Weather is starting to get warm and the seas are calm. Alex and I are back at peeling those damn potatoes, but this gig is going to be up for me in about a week so I'm dealing with it.

March 23rd. The past few days have been spent getting ready for the Captain's inspection. He's got to get this crew in ship-shape condition for the "big deal" upon arriving in San Diego. It's all bullshit because if we happened to get into really rough water again, we would be right back to where we started. Give it a break, we're tired. The line at Doc's grows every day and of course the major malady is the "clap" or "pipe-bending flu" (gonorrhea). Good ole RB was in front of the line; hope he likes his penicillin shots. Thank God, my luck is holding out.

The heat is starting to get to everyone and with temperatures well over 100 degrees, many have taken to sleeping on the outside decks. Icebreakers are insulated to keep the cold out but, with no air-conditioning, the inner compartments are like ovens. I don't know how the guys in the engine room can take it. The heat is so intense, it is making the ocean look like a lake. You can see our wake to the horizon and if any fin breaks the surface you can see it.

March 25th. Well we came full circle today as we crossed back over the equator at 0820. It's so hot that the guys working below the main deck are changing watch every 30 minutes and they are still miserable. It's bad enough just being outside; I can't imagine having to work down in the hole. This will change and in a few days we'll be back to normal.

Back on October 16th when we crossed the equator heading south, the weather was warm but this is HOT. Just glad we didn't have to be initiated in this oven.

March 29th. Just how much cleaning has to be done for this inspection? I mean, really! We are at sea, and when at sea, things get salty. It happens no matter what ocean you're on, it's going to get salty! They're holding GQs, flight ops, personal inspections, compartment inspections, and the list goes on and on and on. We passed an island today and no one seems to know its name. Damn, don't they have maps on the "bridge?" First land we've seen since leaving Valpo.

March 30th. Yet another inspection and this time "O" division sucked. So, just to make sure we ALL get the message, it was "do-over" time. Later in the day another drill was being conducted and nobody seems to know why in the hell we are going through this. The five-inch mount is being tested, for what I have no idea, but they are going to fire the damn thing just to make sure it works. Okay, this is idiotic as they are going to remove it when we get back to Seattle.

During WWII, most all Navy ships were fitted with some sort of anti-aircraft weaponry with the 5-inch gun mount being the largest in that category. This beast was also used for shore bombardments and could hit targets about ten miles away. When fired, they shake the whole damn ship. This is an ice-breaker, not a flippin' destroyer.

So, the gunnery crew is ready to test. The whole crew was on guard and finally BANG! The ship rumbled, roared, and damn near puked its guts out. The vibration was overwhelming and things were broken. That's our Navy for you, you gotta love em!

March 31st. It's Sunday and that means we all get a rest. We are only a little over a week away from Seattle and the time seems to go slower and slower every day. Most guys are writing letters and others are getting ready to depart the ship in San Diego for other duty assignments. Big Don is taking leave and getting married in Riverside, California to his high-school sweetheart. Damn, I'm going to lose a good drinking buddy, but he and his bride will join us back in Seattle after a few weeks off. The big news of the day…NO MORE mess-cooking, so I'm off to being a radioman again.

April 1st. Late in the day we arrived at a point about 44 miles off Point Loma and will arrive in San Diego tomorrow. Held "flight ops" and off went the two helicopters into San Diego. Things will get very busy as soon as we tie up at the pier, so everyone will be heading to bed early tonight. Some have their bags packed and ready to part ways with their shipmates. We will lose our entire flight crew, the research group, those being transferred, and those going on leave. For those guys, Operation Deepfreeze 63 will be over.

April 2nd. Arrived at San Diego and tied up at Pier I at 0800. Started the Admin Inspection right away, and for all the fuss and commotion it didn't last very long. Large mail call and at 1300, liberty was called. We said goodbye to Big Don, and he left the ship in a flash and was soon in the arms of his future wife. We'll get to know her soon enough. RB and I went into San Diego and did some shopping for new civilian duds. What a shock...styles changed so we needed new wardrobes. Not only had clothing changed, but the music…whoa, what the hell happened? Got back to the ship around 2200.

April 3rd. Another inspection today. We were awarded an overall "excellent" and that made the Captain a happy man. Short visit in San Diego and we departed for Seattle at 1600. I was back on duty as a full-fledged radioman and loving it.

For the next three days, it was non-stop drills, GQs, and "man overboard" until we thought the Captain had gone nuts. In reality he was trying his damndest to keep our minds focused. The anxiety level was at a peak and there were bets as to who might jump in and swim to shore. We've been gone over 28 weeks, have traveled over 20,000 nautical miles, and we are ready to be at our home base.

April 7th. Around 1000 we made the easterly turn towards the Straits of Juan de Fuca (sailor boys call it the Straits of Johnny Fuck) and into Puget Sound. A huge sigh and then a roar as everyone knew we were almost home. We will anchor tonight in preparation to off-load ammunition first thing in the morning, then on to Pier 91.

We finally anchored around 1600 near the Bangor Ammunition Depot. Never could figure out why we didn't off-load then and move on so we would arrive in the morning. But, this is the Navy and they have a plan. We'll let the boys think about home for one more night. There was a scheduled arrival and the media would be there, Brass would be there, and awaiting families and friends would be there, on time, as scheduled, so we would just anchor and wait.

April 8, 1962. Arrived at Bangor at 0800 and began offloading the ammo. We departed for Seattle at 1130 and the boat couldn't go fast enough for anyone. It was raining like cats and dogs, weather we would have to get used to being in Seattle, and the tension was stretched to the max. You can see Seattle for some distance and at times we thought the ship was going backward until finally the pier came into view.

A massive crowd was waiting, TV cameras ready, the Brass in their pressed uniforms and smiling faces, wives and children all huddled about and, of course, awaiting friends. It was quite a sight for sure. Hundreds manned the pier and as we approached Pier 91, the band began to play and tears began to fall. We had finally come home.

After the ship was secured, the rush was on to get off the boat. Those of us who were single and had no family there, stood by and let those guys have their moments they had long waited for. Some of us would not get off the ship that day as watch assignments were posted and we would have to wait until tomorrow to renew our adventures into Seattle.

"OPERATION DEEPFREEZE 63" was officially over. We had finished our mission.

It was a sad time as well. We would lose friends or foes. They were being transferred to other locations, and many we would never see or hear from again. Some, of course, we were glad to see go. I would never miss Shakey, Frenchie, and damn sure not Johnston. We would see Fred, Chuckles and Widener leave us and I would truly miss them. I learned a lot from these three veteran radiomen, both in the radio room and on the streets.

Years later, with the advent of the internet, I would be in contact with Widener. He was still living in Arkansas with his family including several grandkids. He informed me that Chuckles had passed away with some strange malady. Unfortunately, we also lost Widener to cancer in 2011.

Both times I got that lump in my gut when one loses a friend. Goodbye, my friends.

The log book I kept on this trip stayed with me for 51 years before friends and some family members encouraged me to put my thoughts and experiences into writing. I thank them for that as memories, some good and some bad, have come back into my heart.

I left on this adventure as a grown-up kid and came back a somewhat immature adult. I had learned many lessons and would learn many more before my discharge in early 1965.

The top country music for the time: Six Days on the Road, Act Naturally, Don't Let Me Cross Over, Still. The Top 40 for this time: I Will Follow Him, It's My Party, Then He Kissed Me, Wipe Out.

CHAPTER 12

SEATTLE POST OPERATION DEEPFREEZE 63

The whole adventure of Operation Deepfreeze 63 reminded me of graduation from high school. One couldn't wait for it to happen, then wondered where in the hell did the time go! When we departed all those months ago, it seemed like it would be forever before we returned, and here we were, back in Seattle. Little did we know that in 105 days, we would be heading in the opposite direction, the Arctic, and this trip was really going to be very, very lonely. Ah, but we have much to do and accomplish before that time comes, and like they say, "there is not a better time than right now!"

The day after we arrived in Seattle, RB and I headed downtown. First stop, the YMCA. We paid for our lockers, changed our clothes and put our newly purchased items away. Then it was off to the bar on Pike Street.

I thought the old lady would cry when she saw us walk through the door, she was so happy! Escorted to the end of the bar, I quickly introduced RB to her and explained that Big Don was getting married and would be back in about a week. She wanted to hear all about our adventure, and I assured her that many stories would unfold over a few beers. We were back into the old routine, us sitting at the end of the bar, and her watching for the cops and Shore Patrol. This would be our haunt for the next four months.

Big Don and Carol arrived, settled into a small apartment, and soon he was being domesticated…not an easy task, I must say. Fortunately for him, she let him play, just like the old days, as she had her job to deal with and would also take care of the housework. She soon would join in on the fun and all of us would share many happy times before the gig would end.

Carol was an x-ray technician and had no trouble locating a good job not far from where they lived. Big Don had brought his prized possession, a '47 Ford pickup, back with them so transportation was not a problem. With her added income, they became a full-fledged, happy couple.

They soon were hosting many weekend parties, and with purchasing adult beverages from our friends on Pike, the parties were always fun. I just wonder how many beer bottles and cans were hauled away from the dumpster in the alley. I doubt they recycled back then!

We were soon in dry dock for much-needed repairs. The one major change was that "cannon" on the bow of the ship. After the removal, there would be additional storage where the ammunition locker had been. This space would be used in our future adventures in the Arctic.

When a ship is in dry dock, everything is checked and rechecked… from top to bottom. The hull gets sandblasted and repainted, props are checked and replaced if needed, the engines are completely overhauled, new equipment is installed, and miles of wires are replaced. Nothing goes unchecked, and things are fixed or corrected if needed. In the radio room, the patching system was completely replaced. This system allowed us to put incoming voice or transmitter signals to desired places aboard ship. A perfect example is music. When a desired radio station was needed in the mess deck, one turn of a switch on the patch-board and bingo! Music to eat by! We could actually patch any incoming signal to every point on the ship.

Each department has its own area of responsibility and will have that area chipped down to bare metal and properly painted by the time we leave the dry dock. The radio room was handed the tasked of keeping the Captain's passage in "perfect" order, the stack deck, the ham shack, and the radio room itself. With this on our list of things to do, we all were busy, even the hot shots who usually sat on their lazy asses.

When the dry-dock work was completed, we steamed up and down Puget Sound until everything was tested and retested. Any problems would be corrected before we departed for the Arctic. Minor problems were detected but did not concern us in the radio room; we were good to go.

Shortly after we entered the dry dock, RB and I headed for Pike to pound down a few brews. Always welcome, we kept them informed of our activities. On one of these adventures we got a bit bored after a few hours and decided to head back to the ship. The shipyards were on the southern end of the Sound near Tacoma, some distance from downtown. As we had not gotten acclimated to the bus system, we decided to hitch a ride. That's when the next saga in this story began.

With thumbs out and all decked out cute in our sailor suits, a red '57 Chevy coupe pulled up and this gorgeous little beauty asked, "where you going?" My reply was, "The shipyard," and with that, she offered us a ride. It took about two micro-seconds and 'lover boy' was in, sitting right next to her in a flash. Now RB thought he was God's gift to the ladies, and after his exploits with his harem in Valpo, he thought he could charm any young thing. Well, we'll see who get the best hand out of this deck!

We were not in the car but a few seconds and soon everyone knew each others' names. Lana was our driver and damn she was cute, friendly, and wanted to party. "Are any of you twenty-one?" she asked. NO was our answer. "Do you really want to go back to the ship this early?" HELL NO was our answer. Then the magic question: "Do you know where we can get some beer?" Hell yes was now the correct answer, and with a quick U-turn, we were headed back to Pike to visit our haunt.

After purchasing a case of Olympia (not the capital of Washington but a brand of beer), we cautiously loaded it into the trunk and were now heading south on route 99 to points unknown. We passed the shipyards and headed west into Tacoma, and soon arrived at a large apartment complex. It was just getting dark as we pulled into the drive and I really didn't pay much attention to our surroundings.

Inside with our case of brew, the radio was turned up and the beers were soon being consumed. RB was giving it his best moves, but this wise old owl just sat back and watched. RB might have been a schmoozer, but he couldn't handle his booze, and soon was not as charming as he thought he was. After about an hour of this action, RB was in a chair dreaming of what might have been.

Lana and I had a few more beers, and we just talked and got to know one another. After a little chit-chat, she decided that we should see each other again...without RB. Those are the words I wanted to hear. She would pick me up tomorrow at 6:00 after she got off work.

She was right on time and, as planned, we went downtown, grabbed something to eat, and went to a movie. It was a typical date, nothing overwhelming, but it gave us a chance to chat and to see where things might go. As dating during the week was a bit hard for her, we made plans for the weekend, a trip to the coast of Washington.

Friday night I spent onboard the ship in anticipation of a busy Saturday and Sunday with this little number who was showing much interest in me. RB was jealous as hell, but he envied me at the same time. And who wouldn't, her being so cute and having a cool car to cruise in. Early Saturday morning, as planned, she pulled up to the shipyard and off we went.

I had a small satchel with a change of clothes and toiletries, all ready for the weekend ahead. We drove west through Olympia and towards the beach. The ride and scenery were like a postcard. After Olympia it was mostly forest and a few small towns until we reached Aberdeen, then on to the Pacific Ocean and Copalis Beach. The sand was hard and the surf a bit rough, not what I had been used to in California. We spent the day just playing around, drank the few brews we had left, ate at a small seaside cafe and called it a day.

We drove back and went straight to Pike Street as we needed another case of Olympia. Loaded in the trunk, we headed back to her place. Again, it was well after dark as we pulled into the drive and I could hardly tell anything about the surrounding complex. Once inside, the music went on and the mood changed. She couldn't wait, nor could I for that matter, to sit down and be close to one another. The music and beer helped move things along and we soon were trading spit, and that can only lead to one thing…like getting a smile put on your face.

Morning came and after a shower I began to study the complex through the windows. It looked very much like a military complex, everything was the same, but these units were not barns. Strange I thought, and as I looked around the apartment, I began to feel like I didn't quite belong here. I was still a bit naive about many things and I soon found out this was definitely one of those things.

The smell of breakfast cooking drew me to the kitchen like a magnet. Bacon does that and I don't know many people who can resist that smell. Soon we were sitting at the kitchen table enjoying the meal and coffee and happy moments and… well, I just had to ask: "What's going on around here? I just get the sense that something isn't copacetic. I don't feel like I belong here." I could tell by the look on Lana's face that she was caught with her hand in the cookie jar and didn't know how to react. She went to the coffee pot, poured another cup of coffee, hesitated for a second, then turned, looked me straight into my eyes and said, "I'm married!" OH SHIT! And I thought throwing potatoes overboard was a big frickin' deal!

I now wondered what look I had on my face, as I felt as though I had just been caught with my hand in the cookie jar. Problem was, that situation could have been fixed very easily. My first thought was how can I get the hell out of here without being shot. My heart was in my throat, I felt ashen, and I had to check to see if I had crapped my pants.

Lana was cool. She sat back down and began to explain the situation as calmly as she could. She was married for sure; her hubby was in the Coast Guard and was on a cutter in Kodiak, Alaska and wouldn't be back for three months. I was thinking, 'Great...now his buddy who lives next door is going to shoot me in the ass! How am I going to get out of here alive?' She had a plan.

Apparently this little fling had been thought out in detail and she was reassuring me that everything would be okay. It seems that this had not been her first parade and she was in charge. Fabulous, now my life was in the hands of an adulterous and I'm in her lair. I can't wait to hear this plan.

With what must have been a look of fear on my face, Lana couldn't help but laugh. "What's so funny?" I asked. She simply said "Everything is okay, just relax, my best friend will be here soon and you'll see." Easy for her to say, but I was not RELAXED! Now I am going to be trapped with two married women!

Sure enough, there was a knock at the door and in walked Yvette. Now I'm here to tell you that Lana was as cute as a June bug but this Yvette was downright stunning. For a second I thought I was in heaven but that thought left me in an instant as soon as Lana spoke.

After introductions, we all sat back down at the coffee table and began to unwind this mystery, and what a tale unfolded. These two were like the Bobbsey Twins and had this charade all figured out. It seems that neither were happily married but they both liked the benefits of being a military wife, plus the challenge of trapping poor little innocent guys like me while their husbands were freezing their asses off in Alaska. That's right, both husbands were on duty in Alaska.

I have to admit that I enjoyed playing house with this little "darling." She was cute as hell, had a quick wit, was smart, and she had a car. What else could a young sailor like me want? MY LIFE!

Soon the plan was explained, and me being a horny young sailor, I really didn't want this to end quite so soon. It seemed somewhat safe once I had the plan figured out. Oh dear God…the price we pay!

She would pick me up at the ship or I would take the bus and get off at the apartment complex bus stop. I would then walk down the sidewalk that went between the buildings and enter through the back door. It was dimly lit at night and she wasn't worried about someone seeing me. I would leave early before the sun would rise and take the bus back to the ship. Amazingly, it worked and no one ever admitted to knowing what was going on. I do believe I aged at least five years those next two months. God knew I was a sinner, a happy one, but now everyone knows!

We had some really fun weekends driving around the mountainous area, taking walks in the woods or just wading in streams. One weekend found us driving up Mt. Rainer. This majestic mountain rises 14,902 feet and is the king of the Cascade Mountains. On a clear day it looks as if it's right next door and it's just short of 60 miles from downtown Seattle. We spent the better part of the day just driving up the winding road, stopping to take in unbelievable views. We finally reached a roadblock; we had reached the icepack. To this day, I could kick myself in the ass for not bringing my camera.

Unfortunately, this little escapade would end in early June for two reasons; one, we finished our dry-dock repairs and refurbishing and went back to Pier 91 on the north side of the Sound, and two, the husbands were coming home soon. The party was over...for now!

We would be leaving for the Arctic in the middle of July and there was much to do to get ready. And, I needed a rest! This playing house was tiring. We would be back in November and could start up again. The next time, things really got interesting!

But now I had to find some new adventures. RB had heard there was some great action up in Vancouver, British Columbia. Soon we were on our way. Off for the weekend, we started thumbing our way north up through Bellingham on what is now Interstate 5. Once passing through customs, it was a short trek into downtown Vancouver. Usually we could catch a ride to at least Bellingham, but often catch rides to the border and even into Vancouver itself, and when that happened it was about a three-hour ride. Most of the return trips would be on the bus as we always had little sleep and usually had hangovers. We quickly learned to save bus fare as thumbing a ride in these conditions was horrific.

Just off the main shopping area in downtown Vancouver was this fairly nice "flophouse." It was clean and cheap, in our price range for sure, and was close to lots of bars and clubs. Over the next two years, I would stay in this joint over a dozen times.

The number one rule for American sailors for trolling the streets...wear your uniform as the Canadian chicks loved sea-going sailors because they most always had money (can't spend it if you're at sea).

The beer pubs were unlike American bars in that they were segregated. There were HIS and HER doors, with couples entering through the HER door. Most were separated by a solid wall so you couldn't see the other side, but a few of the nicer pubs were separated by a railing and those were our favorite. Seeing one another makes it easy to pick and choose, and soon we would be invited to join a few lovelies on the other side.

At 6:00 p.m. sharp, the pubs would close, just like in New Zealand, and that part of the day was over. The next stop was the "club" scene, and there were many to choose from. The clubs usually featured something of interest like dancing, dining and/or entertainment. We really didn't care as long as the bar was open and there were chicks to be met.

Not far from the Hudson Bay Company department store right in the middle of downtown Vancouver was a really nice dinner club, and that turned out to be our favorite hunting spot. Over the next several months, the bartenders got to know us and clued us in on who were the best picks. After clubbing, the next stop would be the after-hour clubs, which opened at midnight and stayed open until 6:00 a.m. These were bottle clubs, a speakeasy sort of place, where you actually put your jug on a shelf under the table in case the Mounties would show up. The Kubla Khan was our choice, a great location and not far from the flophouse.

Friday nights could never be counted on as we never knew when we would get to Vancouver, but Saturdays were full of action. Usually starting with a hot shower, then a good breakfast, and then off to the pubs for a Canadian Bloody Mary, a cold beer and tomato juice...damn, they were good. One or two, no more, then hit the streets downtown as the shoppers would be out in herds and that meant chicks, our kind of window shopping. Lunch hour was a perfect time to find a nice downtown pub to settle into and hope that fishing would be good; if not, the clubs would be next, etc., etc.

Our first trip was a learning experience. We had no clue as to where to go, so after checking into the flophouse, RB and I just began to wander the streets. All good sailors can handle that, and we soon had found what would be our favorite club and later that evening discovered the Kubla Khan. Hunting wasn't good on our first trip, but we now knew what was going on and we planned on going back every chance we had.

With time running out before our departure for the Arctic, RB and I made one last trip to Vancouver. We caught a ride all the way to the downtown area, checked into the flophouse before 8:00 p.m., and headed to our favorite club. Friday nights were great as it was mostly singles night and the action was fantastic. We soon were invited to join a table of about eight people, guys and gals but not on dates, just a group of friends having a good time. A mixed bag for sure, the chicks were nice and friendly, and they all wanted to have a good time. Around 10:30 p.m., we decided to go to the Kubla Khan so we finished our drinks, paid the bills, and headed out to buy our adult beverages of choice.

All the liquor stores were Canadian run and closed at 6:00 p.m., so one must find a bootlegger. This was not a big deal; they were everywhere and we soon learned the routine of purchasing illegal booze. Most were in homes and selections were limited, but if you liked gin, bourbon or rye (Canadian of course), rum or vodka, you were in and out in a flash, all packaged up in a brown paper bag.

The Kubla Khan, located on the second floor of a very large building, was a favorite of many Vancouver residents as it was near the downtown, close to transportation, it always had great bands, offered food service, and mixers were included in the entry fee. I don't remember the amount but it was less than $10. This was a night to remember for sure. Arriving before midnight, we were among the first to enter so we had our choice of the best seats in the house. We were close to the band and dance floor and near the bathrooms. The band soon began to play.

Having already eyed this little 5'1" cutie at the club, Karen, I soon grabbed her hand and we hit the dance floor. The dance floor is like magic when it comes to romance. It doesn't take long to get the message...either you're in or you're out! Lucky me, I was definitely in. I think I found my new love. We danced, we talked, we mingled with the group, and soon she was giving me her address and phone number with instructions to "keep in touch." OKAY, will do!

When in uniform and out of your element, it is necessary for one to pay attention to your surroundings as not everyone is impressed. Actually, some even want to kick your ass just because you're interfering with their action. Such was the case this night. I noticed this weird dude eyeing RB, and it seemed he was not enjoying RB dancing with this certain little number. I warned him to keep his eyes open but when drinking, in excess, one doesn't always pay the best attention to details.

Soon RB headed to the "john" and this guy followed him in. I jumped up and joined just to make sure everything would be okay. As I entered, with RB at the urinal, this guy starts smart-mouthing him. I then suggested his departure was in order and the sooner the better. He left and I thought the coast would be clear. Returning to our seats, I told the group what had happened and to keep an eye on this guy. Sure enough, he approached from behind RB and I, and all hell broke loose.

This idiot, with knife in hand, was about to stick one of us when one of the guys in the group jumped up, smacked him, and he dropped like dirty laundry. Down he went, busted nose, and out for the count. I was later told by Karen that this guy at our table was the Golden Gloves Middle Weight Champion of British Columbia.

Needless to say, the night's fun was over in a flash. A security guard from Kubla Khan grabbed RB and I and led us to the back door and told us to leave as the Bobbies were called and we, being non-Canadians, would be in for a long night, maybe longer. Quickly saying good-bye and "I'll call you," we were soon down the stairs, into the alley, and heading to the flophouse. The thing that pissed me off the most is we forgot our jugs under the table.

I called Karen around noon on Sunday to confirm that she did indeed want to go out again and the answer was a resounding "yes." We talked about the action of the night before, and she told me the guy was arrested and hauled off in hand-cuffs. We planned on getting together in two weeks and I couldn't wait.

Just like before leaving on "Operation Deepfreeze 63," the ship was buzzing with activity, supplies and gear being loaded, sailors being transferred or newcomers coming aboard. One newcomer would become another huge "pain-in-my-ass," a Lieutenant Junior Grade who would become our Communications Officer.

From day one, he was constantly looking for a piece of my ass. I can honestly say that if I ever, even to this day, saw that man, I would bust his nose. He was a spiteful son-of-a-bitch! I will, for the record, refer to him as SPIT. I choose that name for two reasons; one, he was spiteful and S-P-I-T were the first four letters of his name.

We had been waiting for second class petty officer (RM2) who would be our admin guy in the radio shack, two guys that would replace Chuckles and Widener, and a first class petty officer (RM) who would be our crew chief. Two of them came aboard about two weeks before we left for the Arctic and our RM1 was right behind them. The RM2 was still in Japan and was preparing to take a month's leave so we would pick him up somewhere in Alaska in August.

Our main mission for the Arctic cruise was MAPPING. In 1958, the USS Nautilus (SSN-571) was the first submarine to navigate under the Arctic ice. As a result of her findings, it was clear that safe passages under the ice would be extremely useful information from a strategic point of view. Like the waters off Antarctica, depths varied drastically from shallow to near infinity. We would be finding and plotting safe channels in and around areas north of Alaska and western Canada.

All of this action required additional supplies, equipment, and specialists trained in this particular field. With our departure approaching rapidly, the Captain and his officers were getting an edge on so everyone was feeling the crunch. Once we are underway, things will calm down just a bit, at least we can hope.

Big Don and Carol had been busy setting up their apartment and getting to know their neighbors, but found time to have RB and I join them for a few brews and cookouts. Big Don was calming down now that Carol had him under her wings and we all enjoyed giving him crap about being hen-pecked. THAT was not the case, just for the record, but I do believe he was enjoying the new life.

On occasion the three of us did find time to head back to Pike Street and suck a few down. They knew we would be gone for some time and made sure we had our jerky and pickled eggs before we left. Unfortunately, we would all be 21 by the time we returned, and there were several clubs we would explore that offered more than small talk, jerky, and pickled eggs. Sadly, while we were gone, the old lady passed away and Pops sold the bar. We never saw them again.

Mid July came quickly. It seemed we had just returned from Antarctica and now were ready to head north to the Arctic Ocean. We were ready and would stay until our assignment was completed. We all hoped that things would go as planned so we could return sooner than later. But this is the Navy, and anything and everything will always come into play.

The second weekend in July (1963), I headed to Vancouver to spend the weekend with Karen. I made the trip alone and couldn't wait to get there. I got lucky and hitched a ride into Vancouver, then caught a cab into downtown. Arriving around 9:00 p.m., I checked into the flophouse and then called Karen. We soon met at our favorite club, and over a few drinks she informed me that her parents were out of town for the weekend and I was coming home with her. We soon were in a cab heading to the bootlegger, then homeward bound.

The evening was a test for both of us, not really knowing one another. Both of us played it cool, just listened to music, talked about our lives and enjoyed our adult beverages. We called it a night around 1:00 a.m., me on the couch and Karen to her room.

Again, I awoke to the smell of bacon cooking. Damn, that works every time! After breakfast we both took a shower and prepared for the day's activities. She had a few errands to run plus she had plans of showing me around her haunts. She lived in a moderate middle class neighborhood about a mile from downtown Vancouver and soon we were in one of the local pubs for lunch. I was quite the buzz as these folks didn't often have American sailor boys sashaying in with some of their local talent. It didn't take long and drinks were on them. They just wanted to talk and drink and have a good time…we loved it.

The evening was dinner at a local restaurant that served home-cooked meals and then down to the harbor to watch the sunset. Vancouver, like Seattle, is encased in beautiful scenery with mountains, waterways, and magnificent flora. It was a real romantic moment, just like she had planned.

Once at home the music started, drinks were made, and we sat on the deck looking over the city and all its splendor. I wished I had met this little darling back in April as things seemed to be moving in the right direction and it would have been much safer.

Kissing is a funny thing, you flip the switch and the lights go on. Out there on the porch in the night air, cocktails in hand, the moment just presented itself to both of us. Soon the lights were flashing and back into the house. Refresh our adult beverages and to the couch we went. We both woke up with smiles on our faces.

Sunday morning was much the same. Awakened by the smell of bacon cooking, I headed to the kitchen. We sat at the table and while enjoying breakfast, we talked about my pending trip to the Arctic. We both were a bit sad as I wouldn't be back until late October or early November. She would write and would be thinking of me and dream about when we would again be together.

The time finally came for me to leave. She drove me to the Greyhound Bus Depot and I would ride the "beast" back to Seattle. I didn't want the hassle of hitching a ride, I just wanted to relax and reflect, and that's just what I did.

I thanked her for a fabulous weekend, we kissed and then said our goodbyes. As the bus pulled out I could see her standing there, waving, with that sad little face I had just left.

Little did I know at the time, but the world would be a totally different place when we would return from the Arctic. The world climate was bad enough but it would be chaotic in late 1963.

The top pop hits during this period were: I Will Follow Him, It's My Party, Sukiyaki, Easier Said Than Done, Surf City.

CHAPTER 13

THE ARCTIC 1963

The final week of preparations would be soon over. Before long, we would be waving at the crowd of brass, news media, friends and families. The week flew by with final trips to the bar on Pike Street. I did manage a visit to the huge bookstore downtown to pick up some much-needed reading material. I had a passion for reading at this point in my life and was a huge Steinbeck fan. I still enjoy his works, although I have turned to reading history and nonfiction.

Our mission of mapping required a tremendous amount of explosives and with the removal of the "cannon," we had ample space to store it. A trip was made to the United States Ammunition Facility located in the Puget Sound area. (I cannot disclose the location for fear of death.) We loaded pallets of massive canisters of some seriously dangerous explosives. I'm talking thousands of these canisters, which were lowered into the belly of the ship and would later be used in the mapping process.

July 19th. Held flight quarters and received the Bell and the Huey (types of helicopters) with their flight crews. It now looks like we're ready to sail.

Saturday, July 20th. To my amazement, Lana showed up to wave goodbye. That was a total shock, one that I did not expect. My shock must have shown on my face as she soon began to laugh and smile…what a feisty little thing she was.

We departed at 0900 and headed west en route to Kodiak. The whole crew is dragging ass. Thank God it's a weekend. Most will rest, if not on duty, this afternoon and tomorrow. I had the eve watch so after lunch I slept till evening chow. We cleared the straits at sunset. What a view. With several shades of reds, yellows, and purples, God had created this moment for us to remember until we return. Clearing the tree line and entering the open waters of the vast Pacific Ocean, the seas were calm and mild, and the ocean breeze cleansed the air as the setting sun created a glorious picture.

July 21st. Heading northwest into the Gulf of Alaska, seas were fairly calm and temperatures around 60 degrees. Hope is that it stays this way, as these waters can get very rough.

July 24th. The last few days have been boring as hell. Nothing going on, just normal sea duty. We pulled into Kodiak at 1600. Beautiful countryside, water is clear and the air smells so clean. SPIT is being SPIT…a prick! He is trying his damndest to impress us with his knowledge of the radio room. Let me just make this very clear…he doesn't know shit! This is not going to be fun with this moron running around. Our disdain for each other has already begun and I know I'm in for big trouble.

We did get mail and Lana was right on target. I can't return a letter to her as we made no arrangements for that to happen.

We would be in Kodiak for almost a week as the Captain had several meetings with the upper echelon regarding our mission and troubles with Russia. We would be dangerously close to Russian waters and those bastards were just looking for trouble. It wasn't just the Russians that were in the news; Vietnam was making headlines big time and having been off the coast of Nam in '62, I knew full well that things were not going to be good. We could be sitting ducks in the tundra of the Arctic.

Got off the ship and went to the base PX (the government's idea of WalMart). Picked up a few more books and writing materials, and back to the ship I went.

Gipe and I went over one day and explored the countryside around the bay. This was a throwback to what our western frontier must have been like in the Lewis & Clark days. Untouched beauty with streams full of trout and salmon, water so clear you could see the bottom, and wildlife everywhere, including the feared Kodiak bear.

The salmon were spawning at the time, so our two cooks from Oregon went to the streams to find something special for dinner. Gipe and I ran across them, and what a sight to behold. They would cast large silver spoons across the water and quickly retrieve. With the water being so clear, the spoons and fish could be seen clearly in the water. With a quick jerk on the pole, a large salmon would soon become dinner. These delicacies would be around 30-40 lbs. I'm not sure how many were brought back to the ship, but we had fresh salmon for a few nights.

The second day in Kodiak I received a letter from Karen. I could hardly wait to open it just to know what was on her mind. She missed me! Hell, who could resist? Okay, I'm being an ass, I get it. I actually couldn't wait to get back just so I could see her again as she really had had an impact on me.

July 28th. Looks like the meetings with the big-wigs are coming to a close so we'll be leaving soon. Had another letter from Lana today. Nothing special, just a typical letter. She says she misses me. Not really sure how to take all of this.

July 30th. We finally departed Kodiak at 0800 en route to Dutch Harbor. Once at sea we held GQ just to make sure we all had our shit together. I had the mid-watch and when I awoke to go on duty, I found everyone in a panic. Seems there is a Japanese ship off our bow and everyone is having a stroke. I never did find out why it was such a big deal. That's the Navy for you. I had KOMA on all night listening to the latest tunes.

August 1st. I woke up around noon after standing the mid-watch to find the ship again in another massive panic. Seems we are now following a Russian ship and that must have gotten the officers' blood pressure rising. Later in the day we came alongside a fishing trawler and they had women aboard...now, that's the way to travel.

August 2nd. We pulled into Dutch Harbor today and to my amazement, the place looked like Hawaii with beautiful mountains and wild flowers everywhere. We are topping off our fuel tanks for what will be a long journey. This place is of historical significance and that, of course, got my interest going. The Jap's bombed and then occupied Dutch Harbor in June of 1942 and within a month had over 20,000 sailors and soldiers stationed on the island. Their stay was short-lived, and by the end of 1942, they had departed. It seems their major defeat at Midway changed their tactics.

August 3rd. Departed Dutch Harbor at 1100 and are heading to St. Paul Island. As we entered the Bering Sea, the waves began pounding our sides and we started rocking-n-rolling.

August 5th. Arrived St. Paul Island at 0830. At 1300, liberty was called and we headed to the little village for a few beers. Not much here, mostly fishermen, Eskimos, and millions of seals. This island is known for the seal rookeries, which are some of the largest in the world. A bunch of us hopped on a large open truck and took the tour to the beaches where you could see seals to the horizon. We stayed on St. Paul Island for two days, and I was never quite sure just why we were there in the first place.

August 7th. After departing St. Paul Island, we headed due north to St. Lawrence Island. This rather large island sits at the south end of the Bering Straights between Alaska and Russia. Part of the original Alaskan purchase, it is home to a US Air Force base.

August 9th. Arrived at St. Lawrence Island at 0800. We anchored off-shore and soon the Captain and a few of the officers headed in to the base to get all the scoop on what might be going on with the Russians. Liberty was called but I had the watch and stayed aboard today. Being anchored, one had to motor in on the LCVP.

August 10th. RB and I decided to venture into the base for a little beer time. The EM club (enlisted men's club) was huge, offered a full bar, pool tables, ping pong, TVs and tables for card or board games. RB and I played pool and drank beer for a few hours, then headed back to the ship.

August 11th. Departed St. Lawrence Island at 1100. The next leg of this journey would take us due north through the Bering Straits into the Chukchi Sea and then NE to Point Barrow, Alaska, the northernmost point in the United States. Point Barrow is mostly a research station, but acts as a weather station, an airfield, and part-time harbor for Navy and Coast Guard vessels. I'm just damn glad I wasn't stationed there.

As we headed north through the straits, the seas became smooth as glass and we encountered several fog patches. There ice was beginning to show its face and the arctic wildlife became active. The walrus were in herds lying on ice flows, and like the penguins in Antarctica, eyeing us with curiosity. These massive animals are hunted by the Eskimos for their blubber, hides and ivory tusks. Everyone was anxiously awaiting the first sighting of the famed polar bears.

August 14th. Arrived at Point Barrow very early and anchored off-shore. The weather had turned for the worse. There had been a severe storm in the area a week before our arrival, and the heavy seas hurled huge ice flows onto the village, damaging several buildings and destroyed the docks. We were soon told that there was no mail for us but it should arrive later today or tomorrow. Of course everyone was happy with that news.

August 15th. Weather is still lousy, cold, windy, and mostly fogged in. The supply plane was able to land and with it our mail. The LCVP headed to shore to pick up our mail and our new RM2. With the weather being so bad, I was chosen to go out in the blizzard and greet the new guy, show him to our quarters, and bring him up to the radio room.

The weather was so bad you couldn't see the shore, and I wondered if the LCVP would be able to find us. But soon it broke through the fog and pulled alongside with our new RM2, mail bags, and other sorted items. In the boat was this guy in an old arctic fur-lined parka, pulled so tight around his face that only the ice-covered lenses of his glasses could be seen. I helped him aboard and guided him into the ship. As soon as his face hit the warm air, his lenses froze completely up and he could see absolutely nothing. We both laughed as he quickly pulled them off and began cleaning the ice off. Little did I know that this would be one of tens of thousands of laughs we would share over the next fifty plus years. I had just met my Pod, my buddy, my pal...and my best friend for life.

For whatever reason, we always called each other "Pod." Neither one of us remembers how it started or why, but we were Pod to each other for the rest of our lives.

We soon had him at his new quarters and then up to the radio shack. He was in for a shock as he had been a shore-duty sailor for three years and had no idea what shipboard life was all about. He would adapt quickly and soon was swearing like a veteran sea-going sailor.

We would remain in the Beauford Sea area for the remainder of our mission. If all went well, we would depart late October or early November. The operative word here is IF and in the Navy that usually means NOT. We would be looking at nothing but cold water, ice, polar bears, walrus, and a plethora of birds. On occasion we would return to or in the area of Point Barrow and that meant we would at least get mail. Mail is the blood line for all sailors, especially for those in isolated duty assignments. It kept you in touch with reality and gave you hope that your mission would be accomplished quickly. And I had two fillies that I needed to keep in touch with, if you get my drift.

The process of mapping, in my mind and most all others on board this vessel, was very monotonous and boring. Simply put, a hypothetical line would be established and we (the ship) would place buoys along those lines. These buoys would contain recording devices that would measure distance and depth.

Once all the needed buoys were deployed, the fun began. Remember all those seriously dangerous canisters of high explosives? Well, a large amount of those canisters (however many as were needed to cover the hypothetical line) would be lowered to the bottom of the ocean. After sailing away a safe distance, the canisters would be electronically signaled to explode. The sound waves could then be measured by all of the buoys and thus you would have the needed measurements for distance and depth.

The helos played a very important task in these events as they went forward and scouted the area for ice flows that could be problems. They also kept us informed of where the polar bears were. They would, on occasion, herd them towards the ship so we could get up close and personal photos of these magnificent animals. This was also a daily event and flight quarters were constantly being called.

Now keep in mind, this is totally out of my realm of expertise, but I'm not that far off in describing what was going on, week after week after week. I don't really know how many miles we covered, but it had to have been thousands of miles we sailed up and down the Beauford Sea. One thing I am sure of is we scared the hell out of all the fish and game for hundreds of miles.

When the explosives were ready to be ignited, a signal would be sent to the crew (or in Navy talk, all hands) and everyone exited the open spaces and headed for shelter. Once the all-clear was given, BOOM! Within a short period of time, the ship would experience a jolt from the after-shock, sometimes with other effects. If we were in an area that was covered with ice, cubes would be falling from the skies for sometimes minutes. On more than one occasion, when we did not get far enough away, the shock jolted the ship so hard that glasses and coffee cups broke, and light fixtures broke loose from the overhead (Navy for ceilings).

One rule that must be observed when flying the helos in the Arctic was to never go over the horizon. In the 60s, satellites were not being used for most communications, so eye-to-eye contact was required for safety purposes. Being so close to magnetic North could play tricks on ones' compass and the visual contact was a must. This voice communication was accomplished with VHF or UHF crystal transceivers (transmitter & receiver all in one). The frequencies used were established by the U.S. Navy and all operations used them.

U.S. Navy vessels that support aircraft from helicopters to fighter jets require the captains of these vessels to be pilots. Thus, our Captain was a pilot and needed to maintain his flight hours just like a jet jockey would. One might wonder why this information is now being mentioned but it does have a very profound meaning that will be covered later in our mission.

Unlike my adventures to Antarctica, I only kept a daily log until we reached Point Barrow as we would be doing the same damn thing every day in basically the same spot so I found no need to keep a record. I do regret not having done so but the dates (other than a few) really have no effect on me telling my side of this story.

My feud with SPIT was never ending; he just couldn't stop giving me shit. It made no difference what I would say or do; he found cause to reprimand me on a daily basis. Everyone noticed it and I couldn't escape his wrath.

Again it was time for testing for advancement and I was again ready to make 3rd Class Petty Officer. I had studied, I knew my job well, and everyone was pulling for me. With two days to go before the test, SPIT came charging into the radio shack, looked at me, then to my shoes and announced that they were not shined. Now understand this, we are at sea in the frozen tundra and nobody expects perfectly shined shoes in this environment, not even the Captain. I can only imagine what was going on in my head but I seriously wanted to bust his ass.

I, like always, just couldn't let that go. I quickly informed him that polished, shiny shoes were not required at sea. His face got red as a beet and he stormed out of the radio shack only to return in about two minutes and grant me yet another learning experience...another tour of mess duty. He finished by informing me that he had pulled my name from the promotion testing and I would not be able to get my advancement at this time.

Yep, he pulled Jump (radarman) from his assignment and put me in his spot. At that point, Jump and I were the only seaman in our division so there I was in the shit-house again.

Those in the radio shack were in shock and encouraged me to go above his head and talk to our Division Officer. I was perfectly in the right to do so and I wasted no time heading to his stateroom. I pleaded my case and he agreed with me but overturned my plea as he needed to support his fellow officer. And you wonder why I had an attitude.

Once back on mess duty and being senior in grade, I got to choose my specific responsibility. I had had it with those fricken potatoes, and waking up at 0500 everyday, seven days a week, just didn't sit well with me so I chose the scullery room. It was a piece of cake. One hour, three times a day, and I was done.

The scullery was nothing more than being the dishwasher. Metal trays, silverware, glasses and coffee cups all placed in racks and run through the high-powered, stainless-steel cleaning machine. No one messed with me and I didn't have a care in the world.

Located right next to a hatch (door for Navy boys), the cold Arctic air would blend in with the hot steamy temps in the scullery and instantly I would be engulfed in a complete fog out. My now good buddy Pod thought this was the funniest thing he had ever seen and couldn't stop from coming by just to watch me disappear, then laugh his ass off while yelling, "are you in there Pod?" I did have the best job on the mess deck and just learned to live with it.

I continued to spend as much time as I could in the radio shack just to keep my skills at a high level. I was also determined to get the best of SPIT and wasted no time in letting those with the "need-to-know" informed as to the mistakes he was making as Communications Officer. I was not the only one who kept this information flowing as we all had to correct his mistakes on a daily basis.

Late October provided two important events of interest. First, I turned 21 on October 28th, and I wondered how long I would have to wait to have my first legal adult beverage. The second event would be tragic.

Flight Quarters was called on this fateful day, just like most days, only this time the Captain was going to fly in the Bell with another officer (pilot). For the record, since the Captain is leaving the ship, the Executive Officer is now in charge.

Like normal, the Bell lifted off the flight deck and headed forward to do its scouting. At some point in time, the pilot would hand the controls over to the Captain so he could get his flight hours in the books. The day was bright and sunny, the skies were blue, the Bell could be seen clearly and communications were perfect. Nothing seemed abnormal and we all went about our business.

After a period of time (well over an hour), we began to notice the signals seemed to be fading in and out. The Exec came flying into the radio shack yelling that they had lost communications with the Bell. RB, Pod and I immediately tried to make contact with no results. Changing to emergency frequencies, we again tried to no avail. Panic soon swept the ship and the Huey was sent up and headed to the horizon where the Bell had been last seen.

The Exec insisted that we keep constant communications with the Huey until the mystery was solved. He went back to the bridge and ordered the ship to flank speed, and with a zig-zag path we all began to scan the horizon for any sign of the lost Bell. He must have made a hundred trips back to the radio shack, and by the look on his face, we all knew it was going to be bad news.

That news didn't take long to come back; the Bell was down and through the ice. It seemed like hours to reach the spot, but in reality it was only about 40-45 minutes before we could see the devastation. Tragedy had hit the USS Staten Island and a sickening feeling swept the crew and its officers.

Emergency dive and medical crews hit the ice for the rescue attempt. Soon the word from the bridge ended that attempt as the water depth was 1300 fathoms; there would be no survivors. If they would have survived the contact with the ice, the frigid waters would have ended their lives in less than ten minutes, long before we arrived.

What remained on the ice were the two pontoons, a door, the tail rotor and a very small amount of other broken pieces. The body of the Bell became their tomb and will forever be frozen in the Beauford Sea.

Immediately the Exec sent an urgent message and of course there would be an investigation. The orders came back quickly and we headed directly to Point Barrow to pick up those senior officers and investigators, and returned to the accident site. It was clear two things went wrong. First, they should have never gone over the horizon. Second, the tail rotor had broken, flipping the Bell over, and it crashed through the ice on its top. Even if communications had been maintained, we would have been powerless to aid them as time would have been their enemy.

A memorial was prepared and "all hands" would participate. Two newly painted white flotation wreaths with their names painted in black were prepared for the event. All those not on normal watch duty were called, in dress uniform, to the flight deck for the ceremony. It was well below freezing and the wind was howling but we all stood at attention as the Admiral read his brief speech, a prayer was said, taps was played, and the wreaths were tossed into the cold Beauford Sea.

This event was covered by Navy photographers for the "record," and as soon as final photos were taken, we were dismissed. Again the operative word IF came into play. IF everything went as planned we would be okay. It seems that whoever stenciled the names on those wreaths took it upon himself to correctly spell them rather than checking the records first. At the final shot of the wreaths floating, someone noticed the misspelling. The Captain's name was not Mitchell; it was correctly spelled Metschel and so the whole ceremony had to be redone. It took about three hours and we all were back out on the flight deck, freezing our asses off again, just to retake several pictures. I thought Big Don was going to have a stroke and if the cold hadn't made his nose red, his rubbing it sure would have.

We returned to Point Barrow and the big Brass and his entourage returned to Seattle via air. We retrieved our mail, and we were soon back exploding massive canisters by the hundreds. We were now very far behind schedule and had much work to do before heading home.

I finally was relieved from the scullery and back doing what I did best, sending messages and taking care of the radio shack. I was on one of those day watches with Big Don when the next tragedy occurred. Pod was at his desk doing admin work and Major was in the Ham Radio Room making phone patches. It was about 1130 November 22, 1963 (12:30 CST). Major was talking with his contact who was from the Dallas area when he interrupted Major to listen to a radio broadcast…suddenly he informed him that he had just heard on the radio that President Kennedy had been shot. Major came flying into the radio room, white as a ghost and yelled GET THE CAPTAIN (the Exec who was now in charge). The President has been shot! I can still remember banging on the Captain's door and the chaos that followed.

Major stayed on the HAM radio for hours talking with and getting updates from the guy in Dallas. News of JFK's death took everyone to places they had never been before. Here we are on top of the world, not far from Russia, the world in turmoil, and our President has just been assassinated. Our incoming Navy communications were terrible at the time, mostly due to the weather and our locale, so we had to rely on HAM radio. It took several hours before we got any information via official Navy communications. I would guess that over half our crew were scared to death and the rest of us were crapping our drawers.

At the time of the assassination, we were nearly finished with our mapping and we were soon ordered to head back to Seattle. From our location in the Beauford Sea, it would take us nearly two weeks to return to Pier 91.

After passing through the Bering Straits, the weather became violent. The seas were in an uproar and my Pod was in for a big surprise. He didn't do well with the rough water so I became his servant. Those who get seasick will understand; it's not fun and there is no place to hide. The best thing to do is get fresh air, eat saltines, and drink water. Easier to say than do but I kept dragging him out of his rack (Navy for bed) and out for fresh air and always had saltines at the ready. This little adventure lasted about three days. Those of you who have watched the reality show "The Deadliest Catch" can relate as those are the waters we were in. Once through the Aleutians, we headed southeast towards The Straits of Juan de Fuca.

About the 8th of December 1963, we arrived back in Seattle to awaiting Brass, families and friends. The mood was different this time, many things had happened. We lost our Captain and JFK had been assassinated. The world was coming unglued and tensions were at a peak. Many wondered if we were on the brink of war.

The normal activities began as soon as we docked. Those being transferred to other assignments left the ship, new shipmates were coming aboard, and most of us were getting ready for some "liberty." Me and my Pod were heading to the bar just outside the gates of the base for my first legal adult beverage.

Pod and I hit the concrete as soon as liberty was called. We walked in the front door, headed to the bar and I sat my happy sailor ass down and ordered me a "scotch and soda." The bartender looked at me, glanced at Pod for his order, and turned and made our drinks. The son-of-a-bitch never asked for my ID. Well I damn sure took it out and showed him anyway. I had waited a long time to do that and he wasn't going screw up my parade.

At the end of this cruise, we lost about half of the guys who I had been stationed with so there were many new faces and personalities to learn. Pod only had a little over seven months left to serve while I was looking at fourteen months, and I had no idea what was ahead for me. I was hoping I would get transferred to some posh tropical land base but that didn't happen.

In our short time together, Pod and I had become good friends. Along with RB and Big Don, we would find lots to do in the months ahead...some good, some not so good. EJ and Gipe (the ETs) would soon be part of the group and we would share many a brew in the very near future.

The Top Pop hits during this period were: Blue Velvet, Sugar Shack, I'm Leaving it up to You, and Dominique.

CHAPTER 14

SEATTLE TIME

The next seven months would provide much entertainment, and if I were John Steinbeck, a complete novel would be written just about these months. It has always been a complete mystery to me as to how we could cram so much activity into such a short period of time, but we did and we gave it hell!

RB and I made arrangements for 30-days' leave and would be heading back to Kansas City and St. Joseph, Missouri for the Christmas/New Year's holiday. RB grew up in St. Joe and after a troubled family life was raised by a grandmother. His mother had passed, and he had not seen his dad in years. He wanted to make an attempt to find him and begin a new relationship. Shortly after returning to Seattle, RB had purchased a '54 Ford Sedan, so we would be driving back home. This was December 1963. There were not that many interstate highways to make such a trip and rarely could a four-lane road be found; it would be a long hard drive of nearly 1850 miles each way.

Before our journey, RB, Pod and I made a trip to Vancouver. I, of course, wanted to see Karen, and my buddies were hankering for some excitement. Vancouver would not let us down. Pod had never been there and I knew he would just love the action. We drove in RB's car, got to Vancouver around

10:00 p.m., and checked into the flophouse. I tried to call Karen but didn't get an answer. It turned out she and her parents had left the area for the holidays and I wouldn't see her for almost two more months. We soon headed to a bootlegger, picked up our booze and spent a wild, exciting night at the Kubla Kahn. We had fun, danced, met some nice people but no one was getting a smile put on their face that night.

The next day (Saturday) would find us down on the waterfront having our Canadian Bloody Mary's and talking trash with some of the locals. Just about noon, we headed to the nice pub right around the corner from the Hudson Bay Company with hopes of finding a few chicks to hang with, but our luck just wasn't working on this trip. We decided to lay low and put our energy into the night life activities.

We put on our finest civilian clothes for the evening and headed to our favorite club. As we approached, the maitre d' stopped us from entering. RB was not wearing a coat, which was required on Saturday nights. Ties were not on the code, just suit or sport coats. Now what the hell do we do? Go shopping? If we wanted to enjoy the hunt at this location, RB needed a coat, so we went on a mission to find him one. About two blocks of walking brought us to what we would call a "Goodwill" like store and in we went. Pod found the crème de la crème of all sport coats for RB, if only it would fit. Soon RB was standing in front of a mirror, adorned in his new "evening" wear, with a look of total disdain. The sleeves were a tad long, I'd say about three inches, it had large shoulder pads that made RB look somewhat like a hunchback and the length was about halfway down to his knees. The good news was it was cheap and that is the favorite word of most sailors. DONE!

There was a special feature to this masterpiece of clothing and we would discover it as soon as we were seated. RB insisted that he sit in the darkest spot that could be found, hoping that no one would notice his attire. As soon as we were seated, both Pod and I now noticed the rather large embroidered emblem on the left breast of RB's new coat. It was about five to six inches long and about three to four inches wide, and the thick gold and silver threads made it really stand out on the blue coat. To this day,

I'm sure Pod pissed his pants laughing. I don't think there was anyone in the entire club that now did not enjoy RBs new coat. Why we didn't pay attention to the emblem from the beginning is still a mystery, but sure adds fun to the story.

We ended the evening back at the Kubla Kahn but this was just not our time to score in Vancouver. We had fun, as always, and would return for another adventure at a later time. I am not sure whatever happened to RB's coat, but I'm guessing some bum found it in a trash can and thought he'd found a fortune.

Around the 15th of December, RB and I headed east for what would be a three-day drive over Snoqualmie Pass, southeast to Yakima, passing through the southern parts of Idaho and Wyoming into Nebraska. About halfway through Nebraska we headed south into Kansas and picked up Highway 24, finally stopping at a small mom-and-pop motel for some much-needed sleep. We had driven for over two days, changing drivers every four to five hours, but we desperately needed a soft bed before we reached our destination.

The next morning we showered, found a café for some hot food and then finished our last leg into Kansas City. Arriving at my home mid afternoon, we were greeted by my aunt and we were soon at the kitchen table drinking some good home-brewed coffee. RB would be staying with us a few days before heading north to St. Joe and he would be treated to some fabulous meals before he left. That night we just stayed home, and after dinner sat in the living room, telling stories about some of our adventures and plans for the future. My Uncle was impressed with RB and the two hit it off right away. Tomorrow would be busy, so the lights went out around 10:00 p.m.

My aunt made us a big breakfast, my uncle headed for work, and RB and I headed out to see what there was to see. Looked up some of my old buddies and plans were made for several holiday parties. It turned out somewhat difficult for me to adjust to being back at home after being away for over two years, being free to do what I wanted to do when I wanted to do it, yet respecting my aunt and uncles' home. They knew I had changed and needed my space, something I had never really had there before. I told them our plans and I needed to know what they expected from us. Things worked out just fine.

RB was soon gone for St. Joe. Our plan was to be in touch after the holidays to arrange our return to Seattle. Unfortunately, shortly after Christmas, RB called and wondered if he could return earlier as his grand plan just didn't pan out. It seems his dad wanted nothing to do with him and grandma was way too old to deal with a harem-gathering sailor boy. However, he was welcome at my aunt and uncle's home, and he joined me with my old friends during the remainder of the holiday parties.

Time had changed me, much more so than it had changed my old friends. Only a few remained in college. Several had joined the Army Reserves and had spent six months on active duty, and would spend the next five and a half years on reserve duty. They all got very lucky as not one of them was ever called to active duty during the Vietnam era. God had to have been with them.

With my maturity level way out of sync with my old pals, both RB and I were ready to head back to Seattle earlier than planned, but there was a problem that needed to be addressed. RB's car was in need of some costly repairs before the trip could be made. He asked me about borrowing some money as he didn't have the needed dollars. I was getting low as well and suggested that he talk with my uncle. He was floored. I told him that my uncle liked him and respected him, and I was sure he would loan the needed money to him. I arranged the meeting and l left them to talk business. It wasn't fifteen minutes later that RB came back to me with tears in his eyes. He couldn't believe that someone would actually trust him like that, but that was my uncle. RB had given him a payback schedule and adhered to it without fail.

I would be getting out of active duty in just a little over a year so our goodbyes were not all that bad, and my aunt didn't even shed a tear. I would then come back home and go back to college. I was ready this time and couldn't wait.

The long trip back was worrisome as the weather forecast was full of snow storms from Kansas City all the way back to Seattle. It was a good thing we were leaving early as no telling what was waiting for us.

Everything went well until we reached the middle of Wyoming. The snow accumulation was very deep, and farther west into the mountains it got worse. Somewhere in the middle of Idaho on a four-lane road, we had our first encounter with danger. In almost blizzard-like conditions, in the middle of the night, a semi flew by us causing a complete white-out. The draft from the truck pulled us, and RB lost control and into the median ditch we went, backwards. OK, we both had to check our shorts just to make sure we had not crapped them. We sat there for what seemed like hours, not able to drive out of the ditch, when finally a helpful soul stopped and was able to pull us out. We had gotten lucky, and we both drove much slower for the remainder of the trip.

Once into Washington and through the Yakima Valley, we were heading up the mountains, ready to navigate the Snoqualmie Pass region. The snow was piled up at least six or seven feet on both sides of the road and it just kept coming down. I couldn't wait to see Seattle just to get out of this mess. The trip took us four days with little sleep or hot food and no booze. Seattle was a welcome sight for sure and we would soon be with our buddies once again.

After putting all our civilian clothes and goodies in our YMCA lockers, we headed back to the ship and were greeted like long-lost family. It had been almost a month, but we were ready and actually happy to be back with the gang and enjoying the Seattle lifestyle.

The big news awaiting us was the discovery of the world of "house-boats." Seattle is surrounded by salt water and fresh water, and there are numerous communities floating on both. Pod, EF, Gipe and Mac had been shopping for places for all of us to live off the ship. Mac was from Seattle, and knew the city and surrounding area like the back of his hand. The Lake Washington area was the prime area with rentals ranging from completely out of our budgets to being nearly affordable for three or four guys to move into. But we soon found out none of them wanted to rent to "military" types, and we needed to find other locations. That was Mac's job and he soon found something that fit our budgets and lifestyle...which was PARTY MODE!

Between Puget Sound (salt water) and Lake Washington (fresh water), there were locks that allowed vessels to pass from one body of water to the other without contamination. From the locks there was a freshwater channel that ran nearly seven miles before you entered Lake Washington. It was here that we found our affordable paradise. Our little community very well could have found its way into a Steinbeck book as it housed a vast array of characters from all walks of life, and we just added to the mix.

Just north of W. Ewing St. and 6th Ave W was our little ghetto, our paradise. Just across the railroad tracks was the main pier with two branches on either side. Pod, RB and I chose the only nonfloating villa in the community, a two-bedroom beauty that had a living room/bedroom, a larger kitchen, and a bath, all nestled on pilings...solid as a rock. All other dwellings were floating, mostly on old oil barrels that were sealed shut so they would become buoyant. EJ, Gipe and Mac chose a choice piece of property conveniently located at the end of the eastern pier. The porch was sitting right on the channel, and watching the babes on the passing boats became one of our pastimes. This would be the PARTY HOUSE, and the stories that would come from this little abode were endless. This house was much larger than ours but our rent was less hazardous to our pocketbooks.

There would soon be another group from the ship to join us; however, their lifestyle just didn't fit our parameters. It seems they enjoyed smoking funny pipes and taking pills for their entertainment, and none of us wanted any part of that routine. It wouldn't be long before RB thought they would be more fun than us, so Pod and I found another roomie. In the end, all three of these nonconformists would pay the Captain a visit. They became seaman again, and with that loss of pay could no longer enjoy the waterway living.

A visit to the Captain was called "Captain's Mast,"a disciplinary action that could be handled there or, if serious enough, on to court martial.

Once we signed our rental agreements, we began our housekeeping duties. Filling the cabinets and refrigerator with edibles and drinkables was high priority, especially the drinkables, which always seemed to be low…not sure how that happens! We needed basics like sheets, towels, cleaning materials, and candles. Candles would set the tone for romance, the perfect ambiance to lure the ladies. What better a place to shop for these things but the local Goodwill–like store, and what we couldn't find there would be at the base PX store.

Pod and I did all the work for our little home as RB really just wanted to have a place to hang after parties and didn't really want to live or eat there. His choice, but he still had to pay his third in rent and utilities so it was fine with us. We would always make a trip to the PX every two weeks right after payday. Food and adult beverages were cheaper there, so it made perfect sense for us to buy our needed supplies on the base. We soon had our place all cleaned up, shelves stocked, and were enjoying the time away from the ship.

We were located about three miles northwest of downtown Seattle, about two miles northeast from Pier 91. It made a nice little triangle for us to navigate if we needed to hoof it. The only vehicles available were RBs Ford and EJs Volvo, and they would not always be available for transportation. Pod and I soon began exploring the night spots in downtown Seattle. It didn't take us long to find our three favorite hangouts. The first was The French Quarter, a quaint little bar in a hotel at the intersection of Pike and 8th Ave. The décor was very much New Orleans with high ceilings with long-stemmed fans, wild red wall-papered walls adorned with old musical instruments, and low lighting with smooth jazz playing from a turntable located behind the 8-stool bar. Marian, who was what most men have wild dreams about, was the bartender. She was stunning with a soft voice, a body built for two with long legs, and always dressed in what I would call a "bunny" outfit. Good God, I thought I was in love all over again. It didn't take long for Pod and I to claim this place as heaven, and we spent many an hour sucking down scotch and sodas and screwdrivers.

The next place was Gabe's, a small bar just south of 6th Ave. and Pike. It too was a jazz bar with one of the best jukeboxes I have ever heard; the sound was way before it's time. It featured a large rectangle bar with booths along the north wall. Dimly lit, it was a very romantic place to not only take a date but also to find new friends.

The third on our list was The Playgirl Club. Not affiliated with The Playboy Clubs at all, it was just a great place to hang, have a few drinks and chat with those who frequented the club while shopping in downtown Seattle.

These three were the favorites of our group; there were others but these we visited most often. They were close enough to the ship and our houseboat that if we missed the last bus or our planned rides, we could make the walk in no time. At this stage of our lives, walking three miles was nothing, especially filled with booze. Pod and I walked over Beacon Hill many a time after too many hours downtown and needing to get back to the houseboat.

At the time, Seattle was an unknown treasure. It had everything one could want in a large city...spectacular scenery, fantastic schools, great entertainment, and a growing new venture called coffee shops. Hello Starbucks. It also was a favorite of jazz lovers, and many of the bars featured the top artists of the day, Miles Davis, Al Hirt, Herbie Mann and Charles Minges, just to name a few. This city would soon be discovered by thousands and is now the favorite of millions. The expansion enveloped a few of our old haunts including Marian's, which is now where you find The Washington State Convention Center and Interstate 5.

Drinking and chasing chicks wasn't our only entertainment, although it was our favorite pastime. No, Pod, Big Don and I became junkers. With Big Don's pickup and our creative talents of finding things to sell, we had our own little money-making adventure.

On weekends the three of us would head to the countryside in search of scrap metal. Pod, the big city boy from Chicago, had come to the conclusion that if we looked for cows, we would find piles of rusty metal.

And, by God, it worked. Traveling up and down farm roads, we looked for cows and it most always meant a pile of old rusted-out farm implements would be lying around. Not one farmer ever complained that we were taking it away. Hell, we were doing them a favor.

We had located a local scrap metal buyer and we visited him on several Saturdays. It got to be funny as we would almost always be late for his closing time of 2:00 p.m. He would see the cloud of dust from us coming down the old dirt road and kept the gates open.

Two weekends are of note. The first, we had discovered an abandoned stash of old railroad spikes and rail connectors that were of course made of metal. We thought for sure we had hit a gold mine. Loading up the bed of the pickup required at least two beers each, and when completed we drove straight to our buyer.

Once at the buyer, our balloon soon busted as he informed us that railroad equipment is totally illegal to buy or sell. Shit! We had hundreds of pounds of railroad metal. Now what do we do? The problem was solved as we returned the following week with more junk atop the railroad contraband. He knew, we knew, but no one else did. He made money and we had lots of beer money.

The second disaster happened as we discovered a completely abandoned two-story farm house. We entered and found that it had been stripped to the bone; no wire, no piping, no nothing. Pod had ventured to the back porch and located a huge metal, double-wash sink just for the taking. We were ecstatic. This baby had to be worth hundreds. After carefully surveying the situation, we discovered we had no tool with which to remove this monster from its pipes and plumbing.

Being trained military personnel, we were prepared for most anything, but not plumbing. This was a challenge for the U.S. Navy's finest and we were not going to let them down.

Brute force was going to be our approach. The three of us grabbed this hunk of gold and began pulling and pushing and bending and twisting until I thought the house would come down on our heads. Finally, it broke loose and we were set for our next fortune.

As the closing deadline was near, we quickly loaded this baby into the bed of the pickup and sped off to the pay-window…the dump. We made it by a few minutes and we had dollar bills floating in our brains. Ah, but all was not what it seemed!

As the dump-master approached and cast his eyes upon our treasure, the laughter began and he could not curtail himself. It seems we had worked our asses off to remove a 300-lb CEMENT sink. Yes, that baby was polished concrete...and we got NOTHING.

Of course, there were many other spots we loved to visit. On the water front, there were many bars that offered just about any flavor you could think of. Many had pick-up jazz music on Saturday afternoons. Mostly dumps, they were places where one would not choose to drink out of the glasses, so bottled beer was our choice. They had local musicians who would gather and just start jamming. After a few brews, the music became classic and the place started jumping.

There were also the off-color bars that featured same-sex attractions. One such establishment Big Don and I discovered in a drunken stupor prior to leaving for Antarctica. A large bar with dance floor, good jukebox and cold beer, it was a favorite of the local lesbians. One Saturday Big Don, Carol, Pod and I planned an afternoon in downtown Seattle. After a few brews, Big Don and I thought it would be fun to visit the girl's little playpen.

We didn't say a word to Carol or Pod; we just walked right in and picked a table next to the dance floor. It was shortly after the lunch hour and the place was really getting busy. It took Carol about 30 seconds to figure it out and Big Don quickly told her to be quiet and just go along with the joke. We ordered beers and just watched the action going on. Pod had spotted this rather attractive, well-dressed gal sitting all alone at a table on the other side of the dance floor, and he just couldn't resist. A tune began to play that forced him to slide right over to this little lovely, and sure enough they were soon dancing. We could hardly contain ourselves but we just couldn't break poor Pod's bubble so we just let him have fun. He was falling in love right before our very eyes when this "butch" looking individual came through the door and started a fast trek to the action going on at the dance floor. This thing looked like a 250-pound logger just coming out of the woods, and the look on her face was frightening.

Poor Pod still had no idea what was going on. All he could think of was making time with this really fine-looking woman, when the "butch" tapped him on his shoulder and informed him that he was dancing with her woman. The look on Pod's face could have stopped a clock. It took us hours to stop laughing. To this day, he still says he didn't think she was gay. Sorry Pod, wrong answer.

Over the course of six months, there were many such adventures and it's a miracle that we all didn't end up in jail at one point or another.

The time would come when I finally heard from Lana. The hubby was back in Alaska and she was free to fly like a bird. We made plans to meet at the French Quarter and she would bring Yvette. I suggested that Pod would be coming along and she was thrilled…oh boy, here we go. It was instant. Pod was lost to the world. The girls had changed a bit; they were both on the verge of divorce and checking all options, and we were just one of those options.

With Karen in Vancouver and the fun we were having downtown and at the houseboat, I was not really ready to jump back into the married woman program, and Lana and I soon parted ways. On the other hand, Pod had fallen in love, head over heels with Yvette. She would ruin his life for the next few months. There are more stories about this little duo so please stay tuned.

After RB departed, Pod and I needed to find a new roommate to help with the expenses. George, a fellow radioman, would solve that need. Not a pretty package but one hell of a nice guy. Besides he had a car, a '53 Mercury that was not necessarily in the best shape but it got you there. He rarely partied, hardly ever stayed at the house, but we did enjoy some fishing trips with him and he even prepared fresh Calamari from our catch in Puget Sound, which was like eating rubber with hot sauce.

Pod who enjoyed doing art and other such projects decided to take an art class at the University of Washington's main campus. Two nights a week he would head to class, and George and I would pick him around 10:00 p.m., always with a cooler full of beer. One such night, we decided to cruise the strip around the University. Lined with pubs, coffee shops and boutiques, this was where the college action was happening.

Now George's vehicle was not in the best operating condition. The muffler was just about gone, the engine needed a tune up and was billowing smoke out of the noisy tailpipe, and he had more than one light bulb that needed to be replaced, not to mention the shocks desperately required replacing. George spotted a squad car and decided he must exit the main drag and soon made a left turn down a dark side street. I was in the front with George, and Pod was in the back seat with a cooler full of cold beer. We were now heading down a dark street. Soon red lights start flashing. George knew his life was about to end but had no choice but to pull over. The officer walked up to the window and asked for George's driver's license, and that's when trouble began.

The officer looked at George's license, looked at the three of us and inquired about our status and IDs, then pulled out his ticket book. After writing his novel about the situation, he began reading to George the charges he was being sited with, which included expired driver's license, noisy muffler, no lights on the turning signals, one broken tail light and, oh by the way, illegal left-hand turn. I was barely able to keep my composure. George signed the ticket and asked the officer, "how much is this going to cost me?" After the officer told him around $145, George said, "for $145 you can keep the fucking car." No lie, he really did say that, and the officer just walked away. As George drove away, Pod and I opened up another brew and began to laugh our asses off, but poor George never did get over that little event.

Many dates in history have a huge impact on one's life. Certainly Nov. 22, 1963 had a major impact on all of us, but now it's March 27, 1964. It was a gloomy day in the Seattle area, not unlike most this time of year, but gloomy just the same. Pod and I had purchased a huge box of used candles at a thrift store and planned to melt them on a wooden pedestal to create a decorative addition to our living room. It was a Friday night, we had plenty of beer, and the timing was perfect to start our new creation. Music on, beers in hand and candles burning, we began melting dozens of candles, letting the wax flow down the pedestal to create our masterpiece.

It was later in the evening and several brews had been consumed. We were just doing our thing when the house began to shake. Remember, our house was on pilings, not on flotation barrels; this would be the reason we felt the strong vibrations. We looked outside but saw nothing to be alarmed about so went back to our candle burning and beer drinking. The next morning was the eye opener.

Both of us were early risers. We were making breakfast when we noticed that things were not as they should be. A quick trip outside and we soon discovered something was amiss! Some of the houseboats had been torn from their moorings, pleasure boats were wandering unattended, and there was an eerie feeling in the air. The Great 1964 Alaskan Earthquake had happened on that Friday, March 27th at 5:36 p.m. We had been hit with the aftershock of that disaster.

Later that day (Saturday), we were all called back to the ship as rescue operations were underway and the Staten Island was on standby for relief and rescue duty. We could be going back to Alaska at any moment, but in end, we caught a much-needed break. We were not called on for duty as the ship had spent over twelve months of isolated duty over the past 18 months.

The aftershocks had been felt as far south as California and large tsunamis had been created, all by the power of the 9.2 magnitude quake. The damage done would take years to discover as a result of this quake, as it was the second largest quake ever recorded at that time.

The strange thing about us feeling the tremors was we were in fresh water, not salt water, yet we felt more power and had more damage from the shock waves than those in Puget Sound.

In May 1964, there was an event, the Annual Boat Parade, held in Lake Washington that celebrated the opening of boating season. Since 1920, the Seattle Yacht Club had sponsored this event and it drew thousands of boats from as far away as San Diego. It was held on the first Saturday in May just as the weather began to warm, when the air has that fresh smell to it. These boats would pass from Puget Sound, through the locks, and into Lake Washington right by our houseboats. A great party time would be had by all. We needed to build our own craft so that we too could participate in the event.

Not everyone was as excited as Pod and I, nor were they as creative as the two of us, so we decided to build a raft, powered by beer-drinking sailors! Our plan was very basic. There were railroad ties conveniently located at the end of our dock, left in piles after new ties had been laid. The idea was to haul these ties onto our little dock, create our masterpiece, and launch right from our little abode.

Neither Pod nor I had ever carried or attempted to carry a railroad tie about 100 yards but we soon learned that this was not an easy task. They are heavy as hell and full of creosote, an oil-based tar that keeps wood from rotting. We had big plans to start with, but after carrying those monsters to our house, we settled on five. We had mustered up enough rope and began an elaborate weaving pattern that would hold the vessel together, and carry a table and chairs, both of us, and our cooler filled with the necessary adult beverages. We do have to give George some credit here. He single-handedly carried the last tie down the dock on his shoulder. Did I mention that George was built like a gorilla and strong as an ox?

The big day finally came (a week before the official boat parade), and we were ready for the launch and maiden voyage. We had thought about calling the "press" as surely this would be "front page" news. Good thing we didn't, as at the very moment we shoved this very creative raft off the dock, it disappeared into the water almost instantly...never to be seen again! Our vessel must have weighed over a thousand pounds, and with all the creosote, it might as well have been made out of concrete. There was hardly a splash - that's how fast it went down. Well, we laughed our asses off, grabbed a cold brew, and began thinking of something new. It had to be quick, as the parade was just days away.

With all the shipyards around us, there was always tons of debris lying around, and we soon discovered hundreds of plastic containers that would make a perfect flotation. We had plenty of rope left and there were always shipping pallets lying around, and so the work began on our new creation.

Again a creative weaving pattern was wrapped around and through the shipping pallets with several containers expertly positioned under the pallets for buoyancy. Before long we felt like Tom Sawyer and Huck Finn, and with our final touches, we launched to see how she floated. All appeared to be perfect. Friday night would be the big test.

Early in the week of the "big event," boats began filing through the channel into Lake Washington. Each evening we would sit out with brews in hand and watch these palatial yachts cruise by. Pod and I couldn't wait until Friday to join them in our "sailor-powered" raft.

Friday night we loaded our prized vessel up with flashlights for lighting, beer for fuel, and dressed in our best sailing outfits. We launched once again and with our crudely designed paddles, we headed out into the channel to join the parade heading to Lake Washington. Our buddies were sitting on their porch watching the "circus" unfold! Laughing and heckling, and of course, drinking adult beverages, just waiting for the action to begin.

The sun was setting as Pod and I paddled out. We were glad we had flashlights just in case we needed to warn someone that we were there. We continued to paddle and were now out of ear range of our buddies. In the middle of the channel, we heard the sound of a ship's whistle, a scary sound as that meant "get out of the way or you'll get run over." It was a massive barge being pushed by a tug, so we quickly started paddling to avoid disaster. As the barge passed us, its wake overcame our little vessel and things began to happen.

Our vessel was undergoing a transformation that was not in our blueprints. It seems that when the ropes get wet, they stretch and become LOOSE! The great volume of water that just passed under our raft created pressure on our containers and they started to move. The only direction they could move was up and over the pallets. One by one, they started popping out from under the pallets and in less than two minutes the pallets were now under water, and Pod and I were soaked from head to toe. We attempted to use our flashlights but they too had become wet and now were nonfunctional. The only saving grace was our beer was still safe! Still afloat, we had but one choice, paddle like hell and get out of the way. Our little parade had come to an end.

It's a funny thing when events such as this enter your realm. One would think you would panic but not Pod and I; we just opened up another brew and headed for our buddies' porch. Arriving soaking wet with our raft destroyed, we at least were safe and had another fiasco to log into our memories. We have relived this so many times over the years, and we still laugh till we cry.

One weekend I had duty on Friday and couldn't join in on the fun and would show up around noon Saturday. Once in the house, I noticed that Pod had left and wondered what was doing so I headed to our buddies' house only to find that they knew nothing. I waited all day and no Pod. Around 7:00 p.m. I headed to downtown Seattle and hit the joints and was back around midnight.

The next morning there was a knock on the door. There stood Carol with a worried look on her face. "Where the hell is Big Don and Pod?" she asked. I had no idea and panic set in.

Apparently, Pod and Big Don had been sampling his home brew and took off in his restored '47 Ford pick-up and had not been heard from since. All day Sunday was a wait-and-see deal, with Carol finally staying by me so we could just wait. About 8:00 p.m., they walked in the door with faces dragging on the floor. There had been an accident and Big Don's Ford was wounded, badly.

Somehow, and they do not really remember, they took a ferry to one of the island communities in and around Seattle and just explored. After a few stops for brews, Big Don offered to let Pod drive the truck. Big problem! Pod had not driven much in his life, was totally unfamiliar with a stick-shift, they were DRUNK, and the roads were winding. At a "Y" intersection, Pod's eyes went right and the truck went left and into a ditch they went. This all took place late Saturday night and it took them almost 24 hours to get back to the houseboat. Carol was not a happy "sailors" wife, and poor Pod was in deep depression as he had crashed Big Don's beloved truck. Things worked out and thank God no one got hurt. I do believe Big Don may have slept on the couch for a month!

There were many interesting women in our world, some good and some not so good. Mac's sister had an itch for Pod, but he never seemed all that interested. This gal really worked hard to win him over, even baked him pies. She would put them on our doorstep and then leave. I would open the door and there it would be. I'd yell, "Pod, there's another pie for you." Mac's sister was very cute and I could never understand why he had no interest, but in the back of my mind I knew Yvette was always hopping around inside that brain.

Pod was still seeing Yvette on occasion and soon it began to become a regular event on weekends. I had lost interest in Lana and funds didn't allow me to make many trips to Vancouver, so I just hung out with the other guys, and we spent many hours downtown.

One evening Pod and I ended up at Gabe's and were enjoying smooth jazz and sucking beers when two lovelies strolled in. Soon the four of us were sharing a booth. Gabe's was a seductively lit bar that was enjoyed by many of the downtown business employees after work, and some would show up on weekends; thus, our encounter began.

We were enjoying each other's company but it was clear that this was not going to go very far. It was decided that we leave Gabe's. The girls were going to catch the bus and go home, and Pod and I would head to yet another bar. We all left Gabe's and we walked them to the well-lighted bus stop. It was here that we came to realize that in the dimly lit bar, all was not what we had thought it was. After they got on the bus and drove away, I proclaimed to Pod, "...but they looked really good in the dark," and another laughing spree began.

On another downtown venture, Pod and I met these two that just thought we were the catch of their dreams, and after several adult beverages, they wanted to see our little houseboat. It was quite apparent which chick thought I was Popeye, and she was very easy to recognize. Her hair was piled up on her head, clearly about a foot, and I do believe she could have carried at least a six-pack in that mess known as a "beehive." After a short cab ride to the houseboat, we soon had music playing and adult beverages served. Being a weekday and having to be back at the ship at 0800, we had to move fast and they were game. I don't know about Pod, but I thought my night would never end. I had just spent the longest night of my life with the wackiest broad I had ever met. As soon as there was daylight, I was up, dressed in my sailor suit and heading down the pier for our ride back to the ship. For years, every time I saw another woman with one of those beehive hairdos, I had nightmares all over again.

There were many parties at the end of the eastern pier, and people came and went. One such weekend, three strange guys showed up with attitudes. They knew Mac and were looking for him. Strangely, Mac was not around. Everyone was welcome and they joined in on the fun and finally Mac showed up. That's when SHIT began to flow. They had issues with him and wanted a piece of his ass.

I never looked for trouble but, when needed, am prepared to do justice. Three against one is just not right and I told them so. One guy really had the issue so I quickly suggested to the other two that we leave and let them settle their problem. Soon we are at the end of the pier, across the railroad tracks and talking about the moon! Now it's two against one, not good, but not three against one. So I started with my best "sales pitch," explaining that three against one was chicken-shit and they should be ashamed. Things were going okay but soon the third wheel showed up with a busted nose, very unhappy, and joined the other two. Now I am in a bad place.

Once again it's three against one and the one is me! It was cold and damp on the water and soon all of us were in their truck with me in the middle with a knife in my ribs, them telling me what a "dick" I am. Fearing for my life, I decided to challenge them (that was booze talking stupid but I had no choice). I suggested that if they really thought they were tough, we should get together when we were all sober and do battle. I had gambled and it worked. We would all meet on Wednesday, sober, and one at a time we would settle the score. About this time, Pod came strolling down the parking lot looking for my sorry ass. Now it's two against three and they decided just to leave and come back on Wednesday. Damn, I got lucky that night. They never showed up and we never did see them again.

Most all of the parties were great and always with new faces. We laughed, danced, drank, acted stupid and just had fun! Most everyone that came to a party brought something to drink...beer, booze, wine, whatever, and just put it on the table for everyone to enjoy. One weekend Pod and I found ourselves a little low on cash so bought a bottle of bourbon to take. It was cheap, a brand we had never heard of before but it would do for the party. For $5.00, I bought a bottle of "Spot Bottle" bourbon. Really, it actually had a bulls-eye label with an arrow in the center of the target. I made one drink with it and changed to beer. The next morning for "clean up," that damn bottle was still there, almost untouched. That's how bad it was. Just one more thing Pod and I laugh about to this day!

One weekend we held a party at our place as the other guys either had duty or commitments with the opposite sex. The usual group, including neighbors, showed up and before long everyone was singing, dancing and drinking adult beverages. When we reached this point, it always seemed strange things would happen. This night was not any different. Big Don and Pod decided to take a cruise on one of our neighbors "john" boats and before long, they both ended up in the cold, frigid waters. After their rescue, they headed back to the house and into the bathroom. No one paid any attention to what or where they were, but Carol soon began to wonder what the hell was going on. She barged into the bathroom and there the two were...sitting in the old-fashioned bathtub, singing, drunk on their asses, butt naked, and splashing in the nice warm water. To top it all off, Big Don had a white life buoy (it was a wall decoration) around his neck and Pod was playing with a rubber ducky. If only we had had a camera ready for this scene. Carol yelled at Big Don to get his ass out of the tub, get dressed and "we're going home!" And of course he did just what he was told. We all thought it was funny as hell, but Carol did not see the humor at all.

Time was running out for the houseboats as our leases were going to end at the end of May '64. Soon we all would be going in different directions. Pod would be discharged in early August, and the rest of us would be assigned to other ships or shore duty, as the Staten Island was preparing for another trip to Antarctica and none of us had enough enlistment time to make the trip. We would spend a total of four months in our little Steinbeck ghetto but the memories would last a lifetime.

There are so many adventures and happenings that occurred in this very short period. A trip to a local bowling alley comes to mind as does a skiing trip (without skis) to a nearby chalet, but it would be redundant as they all seem to have the same results...drinking, chasing chicks and having a fantastic time. Oh how good it felt to be young and carefree. Of course, there were a few additional trips to Vancouver but with the tension of all of us parting ways, it just didn't mix well with fun. Friendship is a hard thing to relinquish and not one of us was willing to just accept it so freely.

The top country hits for the time: Understand Your Man, Dang Me, Saginaw Michigan. The Top 40 hits for the time: I Want to Hold Your Hand, She Loves You, The House of the Rising Sun, Hello Dolly.

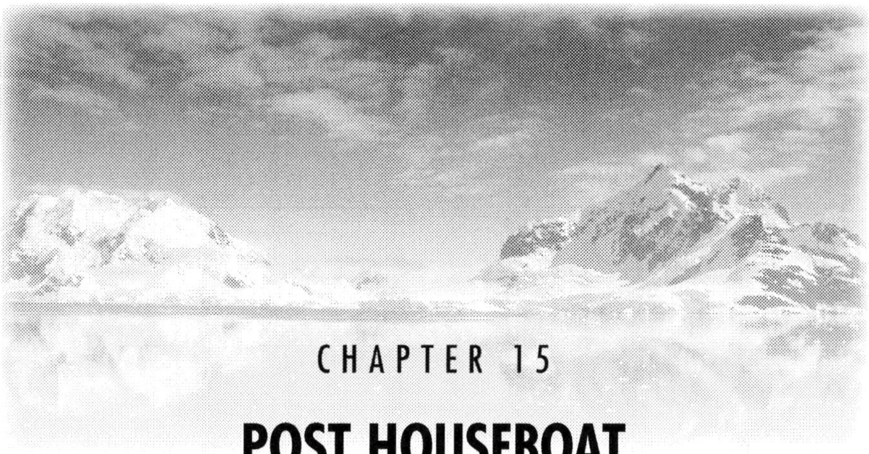

CHAPTER 15

POST HOUSEBOAT

Promotion time was again upon us and it appeared that SPIT had finally stepped up to the plate and would allow me to take my advancement test. The radioman rate was frozen, meaning that not many would get promoted. News I did not want to hear but I began my intense studying program just the same. My only hope was that the test would be mostly operations, not electronics.

SPIT didn't make it easy for me and continually saw to it that I had the most difficult assignments, which allowed little study time. Pod kept tutoring me and was the stop gap between SPIT and I. He wanted me to fail and I wanted to bust his ass.

Test day came and the mess hall became a massive testing center. Given my folder of materials and test papers, I began the arduous journey through mounds of paperwork. I had gotten lucky as it was 95% operations, and after about three hours I had finished. I felt positive but I would have to wait yet another month before the results would be in.

When test results came and posted on the bulletin board...there was my name; LEE RM3. I was one of only five that made that grade in the whole Navy. I would now get a big pay raise and could sew on my Petty Officer chevron.

In June of '64, someone made the brilliant decision that if icebreakers with all their power could break ice and then tow supply ships up the channels, perhaps maybe, just maybe, they could use that power to tow larger vessels on the open seas. Now let's get something perfectly clear here…that's why the Navy has sea-going tugs, and they have lots of them, so why use icebreakers? You got it…it's the Navy's way of keeping people busy.

So, out Puget Sound we went and headed south towards the waters west of San Francisco. There we would rendezvous with the USS Ranger and we would conduct towing exercises. That was the plan but someone didn't calculate correctly just how fricken' much a 1000-foot aircraft carrier weighed with over 3000 men aboard.

Oh, we gave it our all, and most of us just sat back and pissed in our dungarees laughing our asses off. It was what I call a "Chinese Fire Drill." Anything and everything that could go wrong went wrong.

Just getting the tow-line from the carrier to us was a joke. Once that was finally accomplished and it was ready for towing and pressure was applied to the line…it snapped. Yep, broke right in two! After retrieving the parts, the line was repaired, and they tried again. This time we started a little slower and as the line became taut we then added power, then more power and more power until I thought the ship was going to explode. We never even budged that hulking carrier. So much for Navy intuitions!

Well now what do we do…we headed to San Diego for a little R & R. I was hoping we would head into San Francisco as I had never been there to enjoy the night life but Pod's stepbrother, Tom, and family (he too was in the Navy) were stationed in San Diego and the three of us would see what was happening on the southern California beaches at night!

Once in San Diego, Pod got in touch with Tom and plans were made to hit some of the happening joints along the beach front. The Beach Boys and Jan

& Dean's music and beer…a perfect combination. We planned on staying at Tom's for the evening and would head back to the ship the next morning.

The evening went as planned and to this day neither Pod or I can remember just how many beers we drank or how many places we went to, but we did end up back at Tom's place sometime in the early morning hours. Pod bedded down in the kid's room and I on the couch.

I had no recollection of ever going to bed, let alone hearing the alarm clock ringing but soon we were getting dressed to head back to the ship. I had one small problem! I couldn't find my shoes. What the hell had I done with them? We all began searching the house and soon they were discovered in the baby's crib. How they ended up there is left up to someone with more power than I to figure out. Needless to say, all of us had a very hard day at the office after that night!

As we headed back to Seattle, many of us on board were getting anxious to find out what or where our next home would be. Most of our group had just over six months left so any long-term cruises seemed out of the question and none of us were on the list as "lifers" so would not be re-enlisting.

It wouldn't take long for us to find out what the Navy had in mind for all of us. Once back in Seattle, the orders were coming in daily. Big Don, Mac, EJ, Gipe and RB were all sent to the San Francisco area for short-term shore duty, doing whatever one does on such an assignment. Me, I was headed to the USS Burton Island (AGB-1) … another fricken' icebreaker, and I was going back to the Arctic. I couldn't help but wonder if SPIT had anything to do with this. If so, just don't ever let me know as I would surely hunt his sorry ass down and hurt him.

Both the Staten Island and the Burton Island were tied-up at Pier 91 so the move was just a short hop. The only good news was I didn't have to learn my way around a new ship as these two were sister ships and most everything was the same…the major difference was the officers. As they say, they had their shit together and acted professionally. I would enjoy my remaining days in the Navy because of them.

Nothing changed for Pod and I. It was head into Seattle, hit the bars and do our thing. We were spending lots of time at the French Quarter and Pod kept egging on Marian to write to me, as I was heading back to the "tundra" and was going to be a lonely man and needed some female companionship. She assured him that she would take care of me and of course we laughed and thought nothing of it.

During this time the Coast Guard cutter had returned to Seattle so Pod's little fling with Yvette wasn't going well. For fun I decided to tell Pod I had heard that Yvette's hubby had found out about him and was looking for his ass. I had no idea that this would bug him as much as it did, so I had to have a little more fun with a little prank.

We had gone to the YMCA to change into our "city" clothes and I quickly dressed and headed up to the lobby to wait for Pod. I waited a few minutes, then snuck back downstairs. As Pod was putting on his shoes, I slammed my hand hard against one of the metal lockers. BAMB! The sound reverberated throughout the locker room and I yelled his last name as loud as I could. At that very moment, I thought I had lost my buddy. He went completely white and began gasping for air. I couldn't control myself. I was laughing so hard my sides ached for days. We still laugh today about this, but he didn't think it was all that funny back then.

My time for having fun with Pod was running out, as we (the Burton Island and crew) had our orders and were headed north on what would be a dream cruise for sure. We were going to make an "around the world" trek and go places one would never dream of. I would come full circle with two "world" events. What a way to end my Navy career.

Our mission was to head through the Bering Straights, go over the top of Russia and into Murmansk, then to Oslo, cross the North Atlantic and be part of the celebration of the World's Fair in New York, then complete our voyage back to Seattle via the Panama Canal. We had clearance to enter Murmansk, the first U. S. Military vessel to enter that port since 1946, and would finish navigating around the world sometime in late October or early November. We were also going keep our eyes and ears alert to any Russian activities that might interest the Defense Department.

That was the plan and this was the Navy, and we all know how those things go.

The gang was slowly breaking up, and goodbyes to service buddies usually is goodbye forever. I would never again see EJ, Gipe, Mac, George or many of the other guys I had spent so much time with. Many years later I would, thanks to the internet, have communications with EJ and Widener. Pod and I would become life-long friends and are still laughing like young school-girls. Pod and I have tried for years to find Big Don but to no avail. RB came back into my life in 1968 as he returned to the Kansas City area and looked me up. I got him a job where I was employed but shortly after he, his wife and new baby just vanished and I have not heard from him since. Widener informed me that Chuckles had died, and in 2010 Widener himself passed away. EJ and Mac still live in the Seattle area and all of us that are still here are mostly retired. I do miss my old friends, and wish them and their families the best.

With EJ, Gipe, Big Don and RB gone, Pod and I felt all alone so we spent most of our time hanging out back in town just sucking brews. It was really strange, me on a different ship and Pod going through the transition of all the new radiomen coming aboard for the cruise to Antarctica. Pod would be getting out soon and heading back to Chicago, and I would be heading north. The breakup of the gang would be complete.

The Burton Island had completed her preparations for the long voyage ahead and we set sail in mid July. We had many miles ahead of us and I had new friends to make and shipmates to know. The trip would be just like before, out Puget Sound to Kodiak, then Dutch Harbor and pass through the Bering Straights. We would head northwest across the tundra and over the top of Russia to Murmansk. It was at that point in my military life that all I did was count the days. I had become a short-timer and I was loving it. I just wanted all this crap to be over with so I could go on with the rest of my life. I kept asking myself, 'Why couldn't I have been sent down to San Francisco like the other guys?' But that's the Navy and here I am heading back into the Arctic Tundra.

CHAPTER 16

THE BURTON ISLAND

It didn't take long to figure out that this ship and crew were different. They all looked the same, after all it was the sister ship of the Staten Island, but there was a huge attitude differential that I just cannot fully explain. To this day I wonder if the difference had been me; had I changed that much? Was I really growing up? Wow! I would soon be 22 and heading back into the civilian world, going back to college, getting married, having children and making some sort of difference to someone or something. It all was very scary but I felt like I was ready for the challenge.

Our Communications Officer was a Lieutenant who was an Annapolis grad and ended up being one of the three best officers I ever served under. Our Executive Officer was an Ohio State grad, straight shooter who knew how to handle men the right way and always had the respect of the crew, and our Captain was unbelievable. He had enlisted during WWII, gone back to college and was commissioned after his graduation. He was regarded as a Maverick and he truly was. He let his officers do their jobs and he enjoyed the view. He and I would meet later face to face, and he would prove to be the man I thought he was. The rest of the officers followed these three's example and that was the major difference I was feeling.

The radio gang was much like that on the Staten Island. A hodge podge group of guys from all walks of life and with many different talents. CJ was a 2nd class Petty Officer from the San Francisco area, Moe was…well Moe was crazy, always looking for a good time and always laughing. And then there was Tuk. I'm not really certain where he was from but he was a strange dude for sure. I think at some point in his early days someone slammed the storm door in his face and he really never recovered. His eyes and nose just didn't look at you like a normal person. But the funniest of our group was a southern boy, Charlie, from South Carolina. He made Barney from the Andy Griffith Show sound like he was from New York. He hated "Yankees." No one ever pronounced his last name correctly and that drove his southern ass crazy. He really was a good radioman, and I loved just talking to him and hearing his rants. This group worked really well together and we all would experience some interesting times in the next six months.

When we arrived in Kodiak, I could see a major change had occurred since I was last there. It was called the "earthquake" that changed Alaska's landscape. Kodiak, the island, had sunk around 8 feet. The whole island literally was now about 8 feet deeper than it had been prior to the March earthquake. At high tide the piers were totally underwater and we had to wade down the pier just to go ashore. Everything else looked the same but there were major changes that will last forever.

As you pull into Kodiak harbor, one cannot miss the mountains surrounding the area and in July the green hue overtakes you. It is truly majestic and lures you to explore it's wonders. So the challenge was on for CJ, Moe, Charlie and I to hike the monster overlooking Kodiak harbor. With the day off, the four of us made our plans and headed to the PX to gather provisions for the trip. Basically beer and back-up beer. DONE!

The mountain ahead of us didn't really look that far away and it's heights didn't look like that much of a challenge. After all, it was grass covered and didn't appear that steep. So with provisions in hand, we headed towards our challenge, and as we continued to follow the road towards our destination, we soon realized that the fricken' mountain was farther away than it looked. It took us two beer breaks just to get to the base of the damn thing.

Once there, our plans had to change. First, the grassy-appearing landscape was not grass; it was trees and very large bushes, all well over our heads. The gentle-looking slopes that appeared to be almost flat were angled about 45-degrees. We needed a new plan.

Going straight up was one option. The other was a road that looked like it went around and then up the slope to the top. So, the challenge was now on! Two would go via the road while the other two would climb straight up.

We divided the beer load and the race was on. CJ and I took the road not knowing exactly where it went, and Moe and Charlie began to climb. It didn't take CJ and I long to figure out that we more than likely had chosen the correct route and that we would be sucking beers on top while the other two would be laboring for hours just to join us.

Our trip was very casual. It was a dirt road that weaved its way to the mountain and was easy to navigate. But when we reached the top, damn if Moe and Charlie weren't already there waiting for us. They hadn't beaten us by much and we could never figure out how that happened, but there we were on top this mountain with a breathtaking view of Kodiak Island and the harbor below.

The top was very flat, with very little foliage. In the distance we could see a small pond, and we headed there to cool our beer as the water was almost freezing. As we approached the pond, we noticed fresh, and I mean fresh, bear tracks. Water was still seeping into the paw prints; that's how fresh they were, and they were huge. Kodiak bear for sure. The lake was pristine and you could clearly see the fish swimming, which I'm sure was what the bear was after as we approached.

We cooled off our beer in the cold, clear water, then popped a few. As we were enjoying the beverages, we heard noises in the distant brush. Noises like maybe a truck was plowing down trees! OKAY, this party is over! We grabbed the beer, headed for the slopes, and down we went. You would have thought it was an Olympic event, watching the four of us slide, fall, and tumble down that mountain. We all had small cuts and bruises to deal with but escaped what could have been a bear's revenge. We were later told that there was a nuisance Kodiak on that mountain, and shortly after our adventure, the mountain was put "off limits."

We headed to Dutch Harbor for final fueling and soon found our way through the Bering Straits headed for the top of Russia. The weather was fantastic, the wildlife abundant, and we were headed on our around-the-world cruise. What could possibly go wrong? Ah yes! I forgot! This is the Navy.

Like the Staten Island, the Burton Island had sailors who wanted to bag a polar bear and many had purchased their hunting permits. Often a helo would go aloft in search for the white bear and sometimes even herd it back towards the ship. When a bear was sighted, the hunters would be summoned to the bow of the ship and by lottery, that shooter would be allowed his opportunity to bag his prey. This was the most disgusting form of hunting I had ever seen and I have never seen anything quite like it since. I had expressed my dissatisfaction on the Staten Island and threatened to write to sports magazines with my thoughts but I was quickly warned to keep my mouth shut...perhaps I might get to swim with the bears...so I have kept my mouth shut until now. I hope this form of hunting has since ceased. My idea was, if you really wanted to bag a bear, then go on the ice and face him like an Eskimo hunter would.

The Eskimos are the real men when it comes to hunting, not only the bear but also seal and walrus, and they do it in man-made canoes crafted from hides. They will venture hundreds of miles and travel (with no GPS) in parties of 10 to 20 hunters. Now that's what I call hunting.

On one of these "masculine" bear hunts, the ship needed to change position so the chosen hunter could have a better shot from the bow. Engines were reversed and we began to back up and turn when the ship suddenly shuddered and a disastrous sound traveled throughout the ship. We had caught a huge hunk of ice, weighing tons, between one of the screws (props) and the rudder. The ice would not give. The horsepower from the six powerful diesel engines kept on churning, and the rudder shaft snapped in two. Hundreds of miles from the Bering Straits and farther still from any seaport offering service of this magnitude, the radio room became a hotbed of dit's and dah's trying to solve this puzzle.

We were south of the Bering Straits, so that was the direction we headed. After divers checked out the damage, engineers came up with a plan that involved shoring up the rudder so we could cruise as straight as possible. This would allow the two screws to be used for direction, i.e. to turn toward the right. The starboard (right) screw would be put in reverse and the port (left) screw would be given added RPMs. For the novice I know this may be hard to grasp but it really does and did work, and got us out of the ice and into the Bering Sea.

One thing was perfectly clear…we would not be making our scheduled "world cruise." That was hard for everyone to swallow. These opportunities do not come around very often, and in a flash ours was broken.

Now in relatively calm, ice-free water, we anchored and awaited word from the "powers-to-be" as to where we were headed next. Again, there really wasn't much doubt as to what direction we would be headed; we just needed to know what port. That decision came in about two days, and we were now headed back home to Seattle. The trip was going to be a challenge as we would be going through some very rough waters, and with the limited navigational capacity, it was going to be interesting to say the least.

None of us had an opportunity to write to friends or family to let them know, but we did have the HAM radio room. Being the only means of communicating at this point, the pecking order as to who would talk first was interesting. It was all about what you had that was better than the guy behind you. Did you need your uniform cleaned and pressed? Did you want an extra steak at dinner? Perhaps a carton of smokes! Yep, that's how it was and it's probably the same today. Within 24 hours, half the population of the greater Seattle area knew we were on our way home.

As expected, the seas did us no favors. The trip across the Bering Sea was brutal until we reached the Aleutians. Once past the safety of the islands we needed to cross the vast, rough and relentless North Pacific into the awaiting arms of the Straits of Juan De Fuca.

Again, this leg of the journey was a challenge and there was many a sailor hugging his favorite commode while wishing he was dead or begging God for calm waters. Without the ability to use the rudder, the ship had to withstand large waves that hit us at angles and would rock the ship until you thought it would come apart, or made the ship tilt to upwards of 45 degrees, none of which was fun. We finally made it to the calm waters of Puget Sound and were just hours away from Pier 91.

This arrival was not the usual celebration, although many had friends or family member there. Of course, the Brass was there, not to celebrate a successful mission, but to discuss what was needed and when it would be fixed. We had civilian and military experts swarming the ship to evaluate the ship's damage, and in just a few short days, we would cross Puget Sound and into the shipyards on the south side of Seattle.

Those not involved with the "problem" went on with normal duties and liberty was called at 1700. Pod and I already had our plans and were soon visiting Marian for a few cocktails and conversation. Pod would be getting discharged in just few short weeks and would be heading back to Chicago to start his new life, but for now we were just being buddies in Seattle, having a little fun. This unscheduled return would give us few more days to talk about our futures, and we took advantage of the time granted us. All in all, we had about two weeks before we'd be heading out of port.

Pod had finally parted ways with Yvette and found yet another fling. He had just met her and there wasn't much to tell at this time but I would learn later that it became quite a non-romantic, animalistic venture. It seemed that their loins would reach dangerous temperatures, and time, place or circumstances just didn't matter. On one such occasion they were in the kitchen, normally not the most popular romantic spot, and the fire exploded. Yep, right there and then, they got down and dirty on the kitchen sink. I was so proud of my Pod! Glad I wasn't invited to dinner after that episode.

Repairs completed and back to Pier 91, we now had new orders. We would be going back to the Arctic. We would soon learn what our mission was, but at this point it seemed like a waste of time. More supplies were loaded and there were changes being made in the radio room. Our storage closet was now being equipped with newer electronics, and a security door was installed. We also had seven new shipmates, six enlisted and one officer. These guys came from Washington, DC, and all were communications specialists who spoke Russian. We would learn very soon what this was about and why this was of such interest to the Navy.

The day before we sailed, Pod and I headed downtown to the French Quarter and had our usual visit with Marian. We had our usual good times, laughing and enjoying one another's company. Pod kept making Marian promise to continue writing and at one point even offered to pay for the stamps just so I would get some mail…what a pal. Our last night out came to an end and after bidding goodbye to Marian, Pod and I walked back to the ship, about an hour's walk but it seemed like only minutes. Time does that when the conclusion to something good is near. A chapter in my life was coming to an end and I could feel that burning sensation that always happens when someone is sad.

Pod came to see the ship off and again it was time to say good-bye. I knew that when we came back from this new adventure, things would be different. Pod would be free of the Navy and settled back in Chicago. I couldn't help but wonder when and if Pod and I would ever see each other again. I would spend some time with Marian before I was discharged and then I would move on to the next stage of my life. But it would never be the same.

Sometimes you just have that feeling, deep down inside your aching gullet, that things will happen, for the good or for the bad, but I had a good feeling that Pod and I would someday, somewhere, tip a brew or two again. With all those good feelings, it was still hard to shake hands and say goodbye.

Our departure was not the usual big fanfare, but several friends and family where there to wave goodbye and, of course, the Brass was there. At 0800 we headed west for our new mission. One couldn't help but wonder what was over that westerly horizon. How long will we be gone? What really is in front of us?

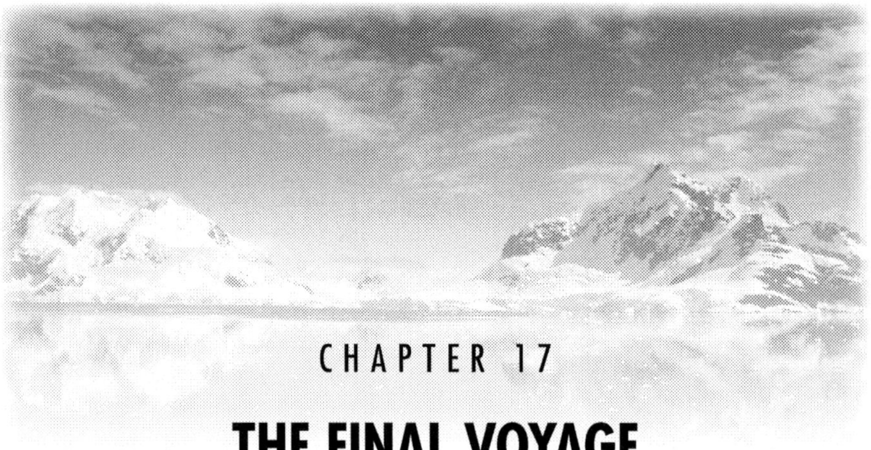

CHAPTER 17

THE FINAL VOYAGE

As we headed toward the Pacific on yet another trek through the Bering Straits and to points at this time still unknown, the anticipation was growing. Who were these new guys? Why were they traveling with us? And for God sakes, what was ahead of us? Things in the world were in total uproar as we had just "officially" announced our intentions in Vietnam. Cuba and Russia were still a thorn in our sides, and I'm sure we had pissed off other countries somewhere on this planet Earth. Six more months of this and I'm back in Kansas City…that is, if we come back in one piece.

The radio traffic was heavy with numerous encoded messages with high-priority grades. That in itself was a clear message to us in the radio room that something was going on. By the time we were halfway to Dutch Harbor to top off our fuel supply, everyone knew that the big news was coming soon.

One evening just prior to the beginning of the nightly movie, the Captain patched into all speakers throughout the ship and began to give us the "skinny" (sailor talk for information) on just what was in our future. The news was alarming and exciting at the same time. We were headed to a location between the Laptiev and East Siberian seas with the sole purpose of locating a Russian convoy of commercial ships and warships. Once located (if they came our way), we were to photograph and identify all ships and any cargo that could be identifiable (missiles and other war-related materials). That was it, short and sweet! We were going to play cat-and-mouse with the Russians.

The Navy was concerned about what military ships were coming out of the northern ports, and without satellites and spy planes, this information had to be gathered the good ole' fashioned way, with our eyes one on one. I must tell you that the Russians were not going to be happy. We were fishing in the wrong seas, but that was the mission and we were on our way.

Not only was the Navy concerned about the number of submarines coming out, but a new nuclear-guided missile cruiser was the main concern. Our top Brass wanted to know everything they could about her, to which ocean she was headed (Atlantic or Pacific), and any other support ships that would be with her.

We were really prepared for this. Fully armed with two…that's correct… two 50-cal machine guns and whatever small arms might be in the armory. Oh we were ready all right, for bear hunting maybe, but not submarines and guided-missile cruisers. It was clear to most all on board the Burton Island that the Brass had decided we could be target practice.

It was also very clear to us in the radio room what these dudes from Washington had on their minds. In their secret little room with their fancy equipment, they would listen and monitor Russian naval traffic and any convoy chatter in the hopes of guiding us to a location to intercept them and complete our mission.

Now with all that information in our brains, we continued on our way, first with a stop at Dutch Harbor to top off the fuel tanks, then north through the Aleutians and then the Bering Straits, then heading west and into the next abyss. Our hope was we would complete this mission quickly and head back to Seattle. Time would tell, and it was not on our side.

In Dutch Harbor, Moe, CW and I took the opportunity to explore a little and we discovered the old air field from WWII. It was in shambles but much of the old metal runway was visible and a few of the buildings, ragged and worn, still stood tall with some pride left in those walls. The mountainous island, lush with wild flowers and green grasses could have passed as being in Hawaii. But it was August and soon it would be covered in snow.

As we passed through the Bering Straits, we headed west into the Chukchi Sea. It didn't take long and we began to have our daily visit from Russian MIGs. They knew where we were and would keep tabs on us for weeks. We did get visited by a Russian nuclear ice-breaker, the Lenin, on several occasions. She was clearly twice our size and, damn, was that thing fast. On one of our "beer" parties on the ice, the Lenin stopped just to see what was going on, so our Captain, through our boys from Washington, asked their Captain to join in on the fun. That invitation was quickly refused and they sailed away. We never saw them again; however, we would continue to get almost daily visits by the MIGS. The days kept passing and all we found were polar bears, walrus, and ice.

One very clear day we found ourselves in the East Siberian Sea, well over 100 miles from any land mass, when one of the lookouts spotted what appeared to be humans on the ice ahead of us. There was nothing other than ice and some open water as far as the naked eye, or radar for that matter, could see. But sure enough, there on the ice were about 30 Eskimos pulling their very large umiaks (kayaks) across the ice. Loaded with supplies, fresh (frozen) meat and their hunting weapons, these Russian Eskimos were 100 miles from land, trotting along on the ice, searching for open water. Now that's what I call "balls." There were three of these umiaks; all hand made from bones and skins, and they were about 20 feet long.

As we approached the hunting party, the lead Petty Officer from Washington was called to the bridge so communications could be initiated. Several of the Eskimos came running toward the ship, excited to see humanity once again. It didn't take long for their head hunter (no pun meant here) to engage in conversation, and before long we were dropping bundles of goodies down on the ice for their enjoyment - cigarettes, fresh water, candy bars, and a few medical supplies. Every one of them was grinning from ear to ear, and they soon were back at their umiaks heading for open water. I bet all they could talk about was "what the hell are those guys doing way out here?"

It wasn't many more days before the clang of bells and the ship's whistle sounded "GQ" (General Quarters). The flight crews were called to the flight deck and all hands manned their stations. The Captain came over the loudspeakers stating that ships had been sighted. Radar had picked them up and we were on our way to intercept their convoy.

Oh boy! Here we go! We knew they were there and they knew we were here, so there were no surprises at this point. Per prior orders, the ship's Photographer Mate headed to the flight deck and hopped into the Bell (small, two-man helo), and as soon as the ships became visible to the naked eye, they took off. Tension filled the air; you could cut it with a knife.

Per our orders, the helo would run the line of ships, photographing each ship and its cargo, weapons and manpower. All of this would be done within International Law, which allowed you to be no closer than "X" feet (I do not know the exact footage) from any other vessel. This would be a major issue very soon as the Russians don't always play by the book or laws.

My GQ assignment was in the main radio room along with CW, Charlie and Moe. We would monitor all voice communications with the helo, handle all incoming and outgoing traffic, and be prepared to jettison everything if needed. That included files and equipment. The dudes from Washington were also in their closet, and the lead 1st Class Petty Officer was on the bridge with the Captain to translate the Russian communications. There was no secret here; the Russians were PISSED!

As our helo ran the column of ships, a very large Russian helo took off from one of their icebreakers. This helo was what we would refer to as a "gun ship," fully armed and ready for battle. Photography was not their plan.

The Captain kept telling our pilot to maintain the required distance and to be damn sure to NOT, repeat, DO NOT enter the Russian air space.

Our little Bell wasn't extremely fast but with the rather small frame and light weight, it was very maneuverable. A good pilot could almost stop it on a dime and turn 180 degrees in a flash. Thank God we had a good pilot as those skills were drastically needed on this day.

The action between the two helos was like watching a heavyweight boxer sparring with a midget. In this little duel, the midget had the upper hand and slowly maneuvered its way back to the Burton Island. Getting back was one thing, landing it safely was yet another. Our pilot feigned a move and the Russian took the bait and Bingo! The midget landed without any problems other than dirty laundry.

The helo action wasn't the only thing going on and many eyes were focused on the guided-missile cruiser. Their crew was busy on deck, and the missile launcher on the fantail part of a ship was seeing some action. It was apparent, even to the untrained eye, that something was about to happen.

With all these things happening at once, it was hard to keep one's eye on any given point. It was like a kid going to the candy store with only a nickel to spend and hundreds of goodies to choose from…just what does one do with that!

The whole "cluster" lasted less than two hours and soon the Russians were headed SSE, and we turned and headed in a more easterly direction towards Point Barrow. We continued to have daily visits from the MIGs but that was the end of our mission, and we now were awaiting orders to head back to Seattle.

With all this action going on, not only did the photographer's mate take hundreds of pictures but most of us with our own cameras were covering the action as well. There must have been thousands of pictures taken that day and some would be worth a thousand words. But we were in the Navy and the Navy always has its ways of doing business. In this case, having pictures of this little circus was not in the cards. Word was soon passed to "all hands" that all film must be turned in for the "official" record. Yea right! I'm going to do that! I had my hiding places and the Navy wasn't getting my film. I had reloaded a new canister of film in my Yashica

35mm, and when told to relinquish my film, I gladly obliged giving them maybe two pictures. The other canister remained in my special spot until we returned to Seattle and everything was safe. I waited until I was back in Kansas City to have them developed. I'm sure I was not the only one who was able to salvage classic photos such as these but many were turned in to the Navy.

The ship was a beehive of activity for several days and the radio traffic was non-stop. Most all outgoing was classified, thus was encoded so only a few really knew what was being said, but one didn't have to be that smart to figure out they weren't talking about their vacation plans. All of us looked forward to the traffic as it kept us busy, so the time passed rather quickly.

We soon were passing through the Bering Straits and now heading into the rough waters once again. This would be my last voyage in these waters and I was very happy about that. I only had about three months left in the service and the only cruises I could think of were in the Caribbean.

As usual the waters were rough until we neared the Aleutians. Once back into open water, the seas picked back up until we neared the coast of Washington. Time was dragging and each day felt like a week. That's what happens to a "short-timer" and I had the disease bad. All I could think about was getting back to Kansas City and getting on with my life. Oh, I would be happy to be back in Seattle and visit my female friends, but something had happened to me on this trip and I was no longer thinking about life with the "payday-to-payday" mentality. I was really looking forward to going back to school and making something of myself. I had grown up and I was ready.

As we made the turn into Puget Sound, the excitement grew to near uncontrollable pitch. Many, like me, were nearing the end of their Navy careers, some would be moving to new assignments, and others would be in the arms of their loved ones very soon.

Nothing much changed as we neared Pier 91. There was a large crowd of family and friends, the media and the Brass. The Brass wanted to view those pictures and would spend hours and days with the Captain and his officers to debrief. Not sure it should have taken that long but this was the Navy and the Navy does what it always does…waste time.

I was back on solid ground and at this point in time I didn't care if I ever went to sea again. If I could have had a dollar for every mile I had traveled in the past four years, invested half of that in IBM or Standard Oil stocks, I would have been a multi-millionaire by the age of 40.

Three months left; how can I make that time go by quickly? Well Marian will help with that as well as a few trips to Vancouver. This is going to be a piece of cake.

The top country hits of the time: The Race is On, Chug-A-Lug, I Guess I'm Crazy. The Top 40 hits of the time: It's Over, Everybody Loves Somebody, The Leader of the Pack, Blue Bayou.

CHAPTER 18

LAST DAYS IN SEATTLE

These next few months will drag along and the time will make me search my soul for many answers to questions I have asked myself before and those that will be asked in the near future. These are times when man as a species challenges himself and it is not always peaceful or fruitful. Time will pass and it will be what it will be, and only God and I are in charge at this point in my life.

CW was married with two adorable little girls and was chomping at the bit to get back to the San Francisco area and begin his new career. He kept begging me to join him and assured me that a job would be forthcoming; all I had to do was choose Frisco over going back to school in Kansas City. That was one option. Another would be to re-enlist, get advanced schooling in electronics and after graduation choose a shore-station assignment to my liking. This was an attractive choice as I was ready to become a 2nd Class Petty Officer and a large (for the time) pay raise would be in my future. A career in the Military was not all that bad of a choice, but Vietnam was in full swing and I had no desire to be crawling through the jungles with a Marine Brigade, bullets flying overhead, with a backpack radio station strapped to my ass. That was, at this time, a very good possibility so this option quickly left my brain. Big Don and Carol talked of moving to Alaska and buying a fishing boat, and they wanted me to join them, but I had seen enough of the frigid Alaskan waters to last me a lifetime, so that too was not an option. My direction was clearly heading back to Kansas City to see what God had planned for me. It was all in his hands at this point in my life.

Marian, the darling that she was, was much older than I and I knew our little fling would soon end, although not without some adventures and lots of smiles. To this day (2015) as I create these pages, Pod and I still talk about her and the other ladies in our lives while in Seattle. I often think about those days as they were some of the building blocks to my life. Maturity is a very funny thing as it never quite reaches 100%. There is always something to learn or something to do to improve our lives and maturity.

I was tutoring a young sailor, Jeff, and that not only included his job in the radio room but while on liberty. He was as green as a gourd had lots to learn, and I made every attempt to quickly educate him on the ins and outs of survival while perusing the streets of Seattle and Vancouver. He was a slow learner but I did make some headway before I headed home. I was responsible for him losing his virginity and with two more trips to Vancouver ahead before I left, I'm sure his father would have been proud of him…he had learned his lesson well. There is no doubt in my mind that Jeff went back to Utah and became a successful cattle rancher and raised a family.

My time on liberty was becoming a weekend-only adventure. Saving money was priority, so if I needed to relax with a few brews and a game of pool, I just headed to the EM Club and drank CHEAP! I closed my locker account, and all my civilian clothes were boxed and sent home. I usually took CW's watches so he could spend time with his family, and would be available for any of the other guys if they had things to do. But my weekends were mine and I valued them deeply.

My last trip to Vancouver was in early December '64, and when I left, I had an empty feeling in my heart as I had had many good times while there and was sad to say goodbye. These things always pass and we need to move on but, to this day, I still think about the good times we had and the ladies we met, especially Karen.

Sometime in the middle of December, Jeff and I went into town for the sole purpose of buying some books. I was a huge reader while in the service and reading was not only educational, it also made the time pass quickly. Having read most of Steinbeck's books as well as many other fiction writers, I had moved on to history and factual literature, and the book store downtown Seattle provided many quality choices.

After stopping at a local pub for a few brews, Jeff and I headed for the book store that was located near the Monorail Terminal in downtown Seattle. From our pub of choice to the store was about three blocks. The sidewalks were bustling with shoppers as Christmas neared, traffic was bumper to bumper, and the atmosphere was festive as the two of us, all dressed up in our uniforms, paraded down the avenue.

Not all civilians respect men (or women) in uniform and you learned to deal with it; it was just part of the job. On this day, five teenaged idiots began to show their disdain for our presence and while driving by, gave us visual sign language as well as verbal abuse. Now, I'm not a fighter nor am I a chicken-shit, and I quickly verbally responded, referring to something about their mothers. They circled the block and were soon back. Jeff was nervous and I assured him everything would be okay; however, five against two is never good, so what was I thinking?

They pulled into a parking spot, got out of their car, and soon were making a scene right there in downtown Seattle. As I quickly sized up the situation, my choice was the big fat slob who appeared to be the bully of the bunch, so he became my target. They were hovering around us, and he soon was right in front of me, just the right distance away for a swift kick in the nuts as he passed by. I could not have aimed any better and kicked him where it hurt the most, then grabbed him, swung him around and into a big store-front window. That ended the action immediately as the other four took off in the car and left fatso to bleed.

The cops were there in seconds as passersby who witnessed the action had already called the police. Several witnesses quickly assured the police that we acted in self-defense, and we really had no issues with the police. However, any disturbance involving military members will always draw the military police, in this case, the Shore Patrol. They gathered info from the witnesses and then took us to the police station to clear us from civilian action, and escorted us back to the Burton Island. All very normal procedure so we had nothing to worry about. Well, at least I thought we had nothing to worry about.

A few days passed, and then both Jeff and I were called to the Communications Officers cabin where he informed us that we were being summoned to a Captains Mast for destruction of civilian property. He would hear our sides and then determine how to handle the civilian complaint.

Civilian complaint? What the hell is that? It seems the store owner whose window was shattered was convinced it was my fault. All of this put us in a bad spot. I assured our Comm Officer that I, not Jeff, was the only one who acted and I would take full responsibility for any of the charges.

A few days later we stood before the Captain and he read the civilian complaint, read the police report, the Shore Patrol report, and then looked at both of us and asked, "Lee, what happened?" I reiterated the whole story, trying my best to miss nothing, and again stated that it was I only who had reacted. He asked Jeff if that was correct and the answer was yes. He then looked at me with his knowing eyes and smiled. He knew I was a short-timer and he was in a position he really didn't want to be in.

Our Captain, our Skipper, was truly a sailors' Captain. He had come through the ranks, just like us, and knew the ropes well. He then informed me that because of the civilian complaint, although invalid, he must take some action. He excused Jeff from the complaint and then asked me what punishment I wanted and offered me choices; be reduced in rank and fined or 30-days probation that would start January 2nd so I could enjoy the holidays or do extra duty. Well, that was a no-brainer as I would be discharged on the 15th of January and had no desire to spend any more time in downtown Seattle. Extra duty it was and the problem was over. If I had had more time left in the service, I could have taken action, which after a hearing, the details would have been taken off my record. The "extra duty" was, of course, a total joke but it satisfied the store owner.

I made one more trip downtown to get my books and I never saw those streets again, although I would spend one more night in Seattle and that was New Year's Eve. This time was on Beacon Hill, north of downtown where I found a tavern that was full of locals having fun and bringing in the New Year. Being in uniform had its advantages this night as I don't remember buying a single drink, and they made me proud to be in uniform. You gotta' love those local taverns.

Thanks, Seattle, for an amazing experience. I will never forget those wonderful years during my time there and the lessons I learned.

January 14, 1965 was like graduating from high school; you were glad it was happening but not really sure what the hell was awaiting you. I had my discharge physical and my discharge interview to attempt to employ me for six more years, and I had said my goodbyes to fellow shipmates. I was ready to head home. Around 6:00 a.m. on the 15th, I was aroused by CW who proclaimed that this was our last day and it was time to get my ass out of the sack! Having been to the EM Club the night before and spending way too much time there, I was a tad slow getting up and heading to the shower. Soon we were having our last breakfast on the Navy and would be heading into our future in just a few short hours.

After quarters, CW and I headed to the ship's office, picked up our final orders, got our final pay, and were now officially discharged from active duty in the United States Navy. Four years had passed, tens of thousands of miles had been traveled, good times and bad times had been endured, life-long friends had been created, and now we were on our own.

After leaving the ship with everything I owned, we said our goodbyes and wished each other luck. His family was waiting for him and ready to head to San Francisco and I was headed to SEATAC airport for my trip back to Kansas City. We would keep in contact for years to come, and in the middle 80s, we once again met in Miami while he and his lovely wife were leaving on a cruise. He had made his fortune in real estate and I was still looking for mine. I often wonder what or where he is to this day as our communications link went dry after that.

All servicemen and women go through these times and they're much misunderstood by the civilian population. Relationships amongst service people are often quickly started and just as quickly ended. These relationships can, and often do, last for years and tie one another together for the strangest of reasons.

To this day, I have tried to locate several of my shipmates and even with the aid of modern electronics have had difficult times locating most of them. I know Chuckles and Widener are no longer with us; RB showed up in Kansas City in 1968 and then disappeared a year later, never to be heard of since; EJ and I have had contact via e-mail and he still lives in the Seattle area as does Mac. There's the one lone sailor whom I have had for a life-long friend, my pal Pod. Oh, the stories and the laughs just go on and on with our lives and adventures since those innocent days and will until one of us joins those who are already on the big ship in the sky.

POSTSCRIPT

February 3, 1961 – January 15, 1965

Those days were so long and yet so very short. The lessons I learned and the lessons I should have learned are now history, although each day still offers new insights and enjoyment. Now my lovely wife, Carol, has finally retired and we can explore the country with our newly acquired travel trailer. We have already made it back to San Diego to visit good friends. Will we make it back to Seattle? Maybe if the good Lord will keep us healthy and our minds alert, who knows where the future will lead us. I do so want to return to Seattle where I changed from a snot-nosed kid to a somewhat mature young adult who became useful, productive and somewhat responsible. Both Seattle and I have aged but we've both grown to be better, and I think we both would enjoy each other's company once again.

Pod and I led similar yet totally different lives from 1965 through 1990. We often spoke on the phone, exchanged letters, and visited each other on several occasions. We both had met and then married our wives by 1966 and each spent the next 25-27 years growing apart from them. Both of us are now remarried to the loves of our lives. Pod never had children and I was blessed with three amazing kids, two daughters and a son, all educated and productive with families of their own.

While Pod stayed focused on his profession in the insurance field, I entered the realm of sales. Pod spent his entire time living in the Chicago area while I, the nomad, went from Kansas City to West Palm Beach FL; Roanoke VA; Des Moines IA; Ft. Lauderdale FL; Minocqua WI; Atlanta GA; back to Minocqua WI and now have settled in Melbourne FL.

It was in the Ft. Lauderdale area in 1991 that Pod and I once again began talking about our futures. He had come for a visit and to finish his SCUBA training in warm water when he informed me of an impending hiking trip back in the state of Washington. Did I want to go? Hell yes, I wanted to go, and so from that point on our next adventures and new future began.

In late July and early August, nine of us started our hike that would take us to the top of a still snow-packed mountain at nearly 10,000 feet. It was on our return to the base camp that Pod informed me he had sold his insurance agency. He wanted to open a bar in the "northwoods" of Wisconsin and he needed a partner. Now divorced, I wanted to get out of Florida and seek new adventures, and what better way than opening up a bar with my pal Pod. I could see the past flashing before my eyes.

And so it was on the eve of opening day of fishing (the first Friday in May, 1992) that The Black Bear Trading Post opened for business. It was a beer bar, bait & tackle store, and eatery all in one; in fact, our homemade pizza help make the Black Bear become a destination.

Many good friends developed and still remain, but four years of that was enough for both of us. We sold the Black Bear Trading Post and I headed to Atlanta for the next step in my life, only to return six months later as something or someone was calling me back. It took nearly six more years before the bell went off, but there she was and now I'm happily married to a beer-drinking, cheese-eating, fun-loving Wisconsin woman whom my children, grandchildren and I adore.

Soon we'll be traveling down the highways in our RV looking for adventure, and perhaps a new book can be written, much like Steinbeck's

"Travels with Charlie." We can write about the people, places and things we encounter, only this adventure will be without our dog, as Ottis, our springer spaniel, is buried on a hill in Minocqua, Wisconsin.

Hope someday we meet in a campground near you. Happy Trails!

In memory of Larry Lee, who passed away in 2016. His last wish was that this book that he worked so hard on, lovingly putting thought to paper, be published.

Printed in the United States
By Bookmasters